PITMAN'S MOTOR-CYCLISTS' LIBRARY

The Book of the
LAMBRETTA
MOTOR-SCOOTER

COVERING ALL MODELS EXCEPT THE "48"

BY

R. H. WARRING

Published by

FLOYD CLYMER

World's Largest Publisher of Books Relating to Automobiles,
Motorcycles, Motor Racing, and Americana

1268 SO. ALVARADO STREET   LOS ANGELES 6, CALIFORNIA

Announcement

We have purchased the U.S. publishing rights for this fine book of the Lambretta Motor Scooter from Sir Isaac Pitman and Sons, Ltd. of London.

The information in this book is authentic and will be of value to the Lambretta owners and scooter enthusiasts.

We also have available a similar book on the Vespa and books on other scooters will be forthcoming in the future.

Floyd Clymer

CONTENTS

CHAP.		PAGE
I.	THE SCOPE OF THE LAMBRETTA	1
II.	PARTS OF THE LAMBRETTA	11
III.	HANDLING THE LAMBRETTA	27
IV.	REGULAR MAINTENANCE	39
V.	TRACING AND CURING FAULTS	55
VI.	DETAILED MAINTENANCE AND ADJUSTMENT	59

    1. Tool Kits
    2. Cables
    3. Brakes
    4. Decarbonizing
    5. Kick-starter Unit
    6. Clutch
    7. Torsion Bar
    8. Gearbox
    9. Final Drive
    10. Magneto Unit
    11. Crankshaft and Piston Assembly
    12. Carburettor
    13. Front Forks
    14. Self-Starter

VII.	IGNITION AND LIGHTING	93
VIII.	TOURING WITH THE LAMBRETTA	105
IX.	THE LAMBRETTA OWNERS' ASSOCIATION	109
	Appendix	111
	Index	113

INTRODUCTION

Welcome to the world of digital publishing ~ the book you now hold in your hand, while unchanged from the original edition, was printed using the latest state of the art digital technology. The advent of print-on-demand has forever changed the publishing process, never has information been so accessible and it is our hope that this book serves your informational needs for years to come. If this is your first exposure to digital publishing, we hope that you are pleased with the results. Many more titles of interest to the classic automobile and motorcycle enthusiast, collector and restorer are available via our website at **www.VelocePress.com**. We hope that you find this title as interesting as we do.

NOTE FROM THE PUBLISHER

The information presented is true and complete to the best of our knowledge. All recommendations are made without any guarantees on the part of the author or the publisher, who also disclaim all liability incurred with the use of this information.

TRADEMARKS

We recognize that some words, model names and designations, for example, mentioned herein are the property of the trademark holder. We use them for identification purposes only. This is not an official publication.

INFORMATION ON THE USE OF THIS PUBLICATION

This manual is an invaluable resource for the classic **LAMBRETTA** enthusiast and a "must have" for owners interested in performing their own maintenance. However, in today's information age we are constantly subject to changes in common practice, new technology, availability of improved materials and increased awareness of chemical toxicity. As such, it is advised that the user consult with an experienced professional prior to undertaking any procedure described herein. While every care has been taken to ensure correctness of information, it is obviously not possible to guarantee complete freedom from errors or omissions or to accept liability arising from such errors or omissions. Therefore, any individual that uses the information contained within, or elects to perform or participate in do-it-yourself repairs or modifications acknowledges that there is a risk factor involved and that the publisher or its associates cannot be held responsible for personal injury or property damage resulting from the use of the information or the outcome of such procedures.

It is important that the reader recognizes that any instructions may refer to either the right-hand or left-hand sides of the vehicle or the components and that the directions are followed carefully. One final word of advice, this publication is intended to be used as a reference guide, and when in doubt the reader should consult with a qualified technician.

CHAPTER I

THE SCOPE OF THE LAMBRETTA

THE MOTOR-SCOOTER is a completely distinct type of motor vehicle. Cleaner, safer and more docile than the motor-cycle, with which it is comparable in load-carrying capacity, its suspension provides riding comfort on a par with that of a modern car. Because of its sturdy construction and low-slung design, which gives it stability and easy manoeuvrability, even a novice who has never ridden a pedal-cycle need have no fear of being unable to control a motor-scooter. These factors, together with the machine's stream-lined, attractive appearance and low running costs—a gallon of petrol will carry the owner 120 miles or more—account for its popularity as a means of travel to and from work, for week-end trips, and for holiday touring. It may be noted that because it is safe, clean, docile and smart-looking the motor-scooter is exceedingly popular with women.

The motor-scooter first made its appearance in limited numbers in 1918, but although, in the early 1920s, a "Scooter Club de France" was formed, the idea did not take a hold on the imagination of the public. In World War II, however, the motor-scooter reappeared, this time sponsored by the Americans for military duties on roads inaccessible to large vehicles. It became, because it could be folded up into a compact, portable package, part of the equipment of airborne troops; it was also widely used on airfields by U.S. personnel for getting speedily to aircraft scattered at disposal points around the perimeters.

The post-war "civilian" scooter was evolved in Italy, originally as an inexpensive means of getting about on roads badly damaged by years of war and unsuitable for heavier traffic. The war, too, had meant that peacetime motoring in Continental Europe *had* to be inexpensive.

Subsequent development was spectacular, and the manufacture of the motor-scooter became a major industry. Businessmen and women in Rome and Paris used them for getting to work; commercial travellers adopted them for covering their territory; all classes of workers found them an attractive alternative to public transport. Some owners logged as much as 30,000 miles a year, often over mountainous country; others used them purely for Sunday motoring. The scooter introduced something of a revolution in social habits and proved itself thoroughly satisfactory over an immensely-wide variety of possible duties.

Among the factories where the motor-scooter was developed was the Innocenti Works at Milan. Here the Lambretta was originally designed and here, to-day, over 3,000 models a week are produced by methods similar to those employed in the major car factories. The Lambretta scooter is in daily use in nearly every country of the world either as an import from Milan or manufactured under licence in Germany, France, Spain, and South America. It has, therefore, an exceptionally sound background.

The influence of the motor-scooter soon spread outside the Continent, but in this country it was at first regarded with some scepticism, for it was felt that our climate made "open" motoring a somewhat doubtful pleasure. The results, however, have been as spectacular as they were on the Continent; over 100,000 scooters of all categories were licensed in 1956 and their numbers continue to grow rapidly.

The introduction of the motor-scooter to this country has, nevertheless, not been without its troubles. While the larger British motor-cycle manufacturers have in the past stood aloof from this field, and continue to do so, smaller firms, attracted to what was, and still is, a vast potential market have, after a limited production, for one reason or another closed down and left their customers without spares or servicing facilities. One result of this is that the market has been largely dominated by foreign designs, and where foreign machines are imported there is generally difficulty in obtaining spares and skilled servicing.

British Lambretta Concessionaires. All Lambrettas in this country have been imported direct from the parent company through the British-owned company Lambretta Concessionaires, who are responsible for the spares and servicing facilities available to all British Lambretta owners.

The British Lambretta Concessionaires imported their first Lambretta models in 1952, these being the then current production model C. Import on a far larger scale developed throughout 1953-4 with demand far exceeding the anticipated figures and planned service facilities. By the end of that year it became obvious that, in regard to spares and servicing, a complete revision of planning was necessary. This culminated, in mid-1956, in the extension and complete re-equipment of the main servicing station at Wimbledon and, throughout the country, the establishment of accredited agents equipped and trained to undertake Lambretta servicing and repair as well as to carry a comprehensive range of spares. At the same time a "replacement unit" service was established, a service similar to that common in the car industry where old or worn units or complete assemblies can be exchanged for guaranteed replacements at substantially less cost than factory-new items.

Exchange units are reconditioned at the British works but all spares, together with the complete machines, are imported from Italy. The holding stock of spares is maintained at a level considerably in excess of any likely demand, the spares being as readily available to the British customer, through the Lambretta agents, as those of any product manufactured completely in this country.

LAMBRETTA MODELS

The first production Lambretta was the Model A but although this was sold in some numbers in Italy no machines of this type were imported into this country. It was, basically, a "utility" type of scooter. The Model B which followed, featured coil springing and knuckle-joint rear suspension. The 123 c.c. engine was fitted to one end of a central girder-frame with the steering unit suspended, parallelogram fashion, at the other. Double tubes bent around the tank and over the engine, supporting the driver's seat and pillion seat. It is estimated that no more than five of these machines were imported into this country.

The Model C, Fig. 1, which appeared in 1952, retained the same 123 c.c

FIG. 1. MODEL C LAMBRETTA WITH THE EARLY SUSPENSION SYSTEM
The back wheel is sprung independently of the transmission case. The front compression springs are housed in cylindrical members attached to the front of the forks.

engine as the B but introduced the single-tube frame which has since continued. The engine block was made integral with the frame, rear suspension being achieved by a spring compressed by an axial tie-rod and affecting the immediate back wheel assembly. The shaft bevel drive terminated in a reduction gear coupling to the rear wheel, permitting displacement of the wheel independent of the fixed transmission case. It was a characteristic of these machines that letting in the clutch produced a torque reaction on the suspension which caused the rear of the machine to lift on pulling away from a standing start.

The Model C introduced a further feature common on later models, the LC version, an essentially similar machine to the C but with side panels,

FIG. 2. MODEL D LAMBRETTA WITH 125 C.C. ENGINE
Torsion-bar rear suspension introduced and the rear brake is now cable-operated.

FIG. 3. 150 C.C. D AND LD MODELS
Illustrating the basic difference in appearance. Although an "open" type the 150 c.c. engine on the D model is cowled.

encasing the rear and body fairings, extending up to the dashboard. The Model C had foot-boards sweeping up only as far as the bottom bearing of the front forks. In subsequent models the L appendage to the model, designates the covered, faired-in version.

A detail difference between Models C and LC was that the flywheel of the C engine had a plain face with the necessary cooling air draught over the engine achieved by forward motion of the machine. Enclosing the

FIG. 4. A 125 c.c. MODEL LD

A hinged panel on the right-hand fairing panel gives access to the carburettor controls. Compare with Fig. 19 (*a*) for other differences.

engine with side panels made it necessary to introduce forced draught cooling on the LC model. To achieve this the flywheel periphery was cast in the form of fan blades and the engine itself shrouded with a light-metal shield giving a direct and positive airflow over the cylinder fins independent of any forward motion of the machine and dependent only on engine speed. All Models C and LC had rod-operated rear brake linkage.

The Model D, Fig. 2, appeared in 1953, its main difference being the incorporation of torsion-bar rear suspension in which the whole engine-transmission unit was pivotally mounted and "sprung" by linkage to a torsion bar. This materially improved the ride characteristics. The Model

LD, which appeared at the same time, had the rear encased and extended leg-shield fairings similar to the LC.

The D and LD with the 123 c.c. engine were imported into this country in considerable numbers during 1953–55, the faired-in version (LD) being generally more popular. Following the introduction of the D models the Lambretta was made available with two engine sizes, the improved performance of the 150 c.c. engine being justified for better load-carrying such as two-up for touring, etc. From April, 1955, onwards, only the 150 c.c.

Fig. 5. The Lambretta Adapted for Sidecar Work

The sidecar has a capacity for one adult and a child carried on the knee. A revised gearbox with lower ratios is essential as part of the conversion.

D and LD models, Fig. 3, have been imported into this country, the latter being by far the more numerous. Production of the 125 c.c. D model and LD, Fig. 4, actually ceased in Italy in February, 1955. During the latter part of 1956, however, a new 125 c.c. model appeared with a limited production, essentially similar to the later 150 c.c. D and LD models with the exception of the reduced-capacity engine. No models of this type were scheduled for import into this country during 1956–7.

Before going out of production, the original 125 c.c. LD model appeared in several forms with self-starter motors, the variations being largely a matter of differences in the charging circuit. The self-starter model imported into this country (1956 on) is the 150 c.c. Model LDA with a 12-volt battery and direct current electrical circuit. Some of the earlier 150 c.c. self-starter models had 6-volt battery circuits.

The Model LDB is essentially a standard LD machine with the addition of battery parking lights, and standard LD or D machines can be adapted to this (*see* Chapter VII). During the years of production since 1953 there

FIG. 6. COMMERCIAL SIDE-CARRIER ADAPTED TO A STANDARD 150 LD MODEL, BUT AGAIN WITH "SIDECAR" GEARBOX

have also been numerous small improvements introduced on the D and LD series models, such as in the design of the silencer, on the methods of adjusting the cables, the position of the kick-starter pedal, etc. There are also several detail differences between the D and LD machines, and the 125 c.c. and 150 c.c. machines of each type. Where significant, these are described in the maintenance sections.

The Lambretta can also be adapted for sidecar work, Fig. 5, either with a passenger sidecar, Fig. 5, or a box-carrier, Fig. 6, for commercial duties. Capacity of the recommended passenger sidecar is one adult with space to carry a child on the knee, carrier weight not to exceed 224 lb. Recommended dimensions for the commercial carrier are 4 ft 9 in. × 16 in. × 16 in. and maximum empty weight 150 lb.

Conversion can be adapted to any of the D or LD models although the 150 c.c. engine is obviously to be preferred on account of the extra weight to be carried, which may also include a pillion passenger. It is also strongly recommended that reduced gear ratios be employed. A special gearbox for this purpose is available, fitted either to new machines ordered specifically for sidecar work, or as a conversion unit for adapting standard machines to take a sidecar.

CHARACTERISTICS

Motor-scooters, as a class, range in size from the near-bicycle with engines of 50 c.c. to 100 c.c. to the near-motor-cycle with engines of 200 c.c. or more. The 150 c.c. engine compromises between motor-cycle performance and carrying capacity with the economy of the smaller engine. It is a little on the marginal side for accommodating sidecar loads but a characteristic of a two-stroke engine is that it is most efficient when working hardest. Such penalties as increased wear, higher fuel consumption, lower acceleration and reduced overall performance are, however, inescapable consequences.

One of the most surprising features of the Lambretta is its weight. Unladen, the Model D weighs 165 lb and Model LD 194 lb, which is considerably higher than one would expect at first glance. It should be pointed out, however, that it is only about two-thirds the weight of the average large motor-scooter and only about half the weight of a motor-cycle of comparable power. It is this weight, largely centred low down, coupled with its small wheel-diameter which gives the Lambretta its exceptional stability and makes it even more manoeuvrable at very low speeds than a bicycle. At a more moderate speed, say about 10 m.p.h., the machine does literally "settle in a groove" with a most positive feeling of safety even on treacherous surfaces. The small wheel-diameter is also responsible for excellent acceleration.

Top speed for the 150 c.c. D and LD is approximately 45 m.p.h. with a cruising speed of 35 m.p.h. These figures vary somewhat with individual machines and how the engine has been treated during the running-in period. Fuel consumption at around cruising speed is of the order of 100–120 m.p.g. The Model D has a standard tank capacity of 1·4 gal and the Model LD a capacity of 1·55 gal with a reserve in each case of 1·25 pints. Thus, if the main tank "runs dry," switching over to reserve provides enough fuel to cover a further distance of some ten miles. Fuel required is standard grade petrol mixed with SAE 30 grade lubricating oil in the ratio of half a pint of oil per gal of petrol. (*See also* Chapter III.)

For taxation purposes the Lambretta is classed as a 150 c.c. bicycle with an annual rate of 17s. 6d. (1956). Insurance charges will vary with the type of coverage required and, to some extent, the status and experience of the applicant. A minimum Third Party Insurance coverage is obligatory by statute before the vehicle can legally be driven on the roads. Drivers must also hold a current driving licence endorsed for category G, or failing this a provisional licence (which necessitates the display of L plates on the machine). Drivers with a provisional licence only, may not carry a pillion passenger unless that passenger holds a current category G driving licence.

Overall running costs of a Lambretta should average about one penny per mile or, roughly, half the cost of travel by public transport. Fuel alone costs about a halfpenny a mile. Experience has also shown that the Lambretta is an extremely reliable machine which, if regularly maintained, should have a useful life comparable with that of a motor car. A 1956 owner-census by Innocenti of machines produced originally in 1945–6 showed that numerous users had established mileage figures of between 60,000 and 100,000 miles on the original engine, with the highest figure logged at 146,000 miles.

EQUIPMENT AND FITTINGS

All machines are supplied as basic models with the following standard fittings—

Model LD—driving lights—speedometer—driver's seat

Model D—driving lights—speedometer—driver's seat

Model LDA—driving lights—electric starter—parking lights—speedometer—driver's seat.

Available as extra items is a wide range of accessories. All 150 c.c. models, for example, are fitted with a shock-absorber on the rear suspension as standard. Some 125 c.c. models have a mounting lug on the transmission case for the attachment of a shock absorber as an extra (although there is no similar lug on the frame); while special shock absorber units for 125 c.c. models have been produced as an extra item. No 125 c.c. machines have shock absorbers fitted as standard.

Pillion seats and spare wheels are available for all models, with various carrier attachments to take the spare wheel and, if required, a spare petrol tank. Side panels are available for covering in the Model D. Bumpers, grilles, heel plates, etc., are made for LD models. Various forms of windscreens are available for all models, together with mackintosh covers, driving aprons, panniers, etc.

The range is far too comprehensive to describe in detail but some typical applications can be gleaned from a study of the photographs. Largely they can be sub-divided into three main categories: functional, aesthetic and luxury additions. Of the functional accessories a windscreen is generally considered a necessity. This should be adjusted with the top roughly just below eye level so that the body is completely shielded but allowing direct vision should the screen become obscured, as when following another vehicle on a wet road. Addition of a rear shock absorber, where not fitted as standard, materially improves the ride comfort, particularly if the machine is to be operated over rough roads. A rear-view mirror attached to the handlebars can make for safer driving although it is commonly a characteristic of such fittings that they tend to vibrate, with impaired efficiency, as well as being something of a distraction at times.

A spare wheel is always a wise "extra," although if stranded with a puncture and no spare the offending wheel can readily be taken off and carried to the nearest garage. The fitment of pillion seat, carriers, etc., will largely be dictated by the duties required from the machine. The aesthetic and luxury items will most likely be dictated by the depth of the owner's pocket.

Suggested Useful Extras. Spare wheel and carrier, pillion seat, windscreen, pillion footboards (a pillion footrest is an essential extra item on the D model when carrying a pillion passenger), front pannier.

Colour Schemes. Before mid-1956 all Lambrettas from the Innocenti Works in Milan were finished all over in Lambretta grey, except for the standard chrome-plated parts, etc. From early 1955 onwards, panels have been re-sprayed in this country to give a variety of colour schemes, any particular colour or colour scheme being available at the customer's request at extra cost.

From mid-1956 the Milan production has turned out batches of coloured LD models at the standard price, the alternative schemes being grey and red, grey and blue, grey and green. The darker colour in each case is applicable to the side panels. Standard colour scheme for all LDA (self-starter) models is blue side panels and blue front and trim, the remainder being Lambretta grey.

Parking. For the purpose of parking facilities and charges, the Lambretta is classed as a motor bicycle and similar rates apply. For freight charges relating to road, rail or air delivery, current charges are best checked with the authorities concerned. These will differ by a large margin according to whether the vehicle is accompanied or not, and if it is not accompanied, whether sent at owner's or carriers' risk. Rates are generally cheaper per mile the greater the distance involved. For rail transport, accompanied, the rate is likely to work out at about the same as single-journey second-class passenger fare.

CHAPTER II

PARTS OF THE LAMBRETTA

SURPRISINGLY, a great many Lambretta owners are not mechanically minded—that is true also for most scooter owners—and when they own their first machines they may not even know what a sparking plug is. This has no bearing at all on their driving ability, or on the enjoyment they may get from their machine. But no machine, however good, can be completely foolproof and so will need some attention to its mechanical parts from time to time. This, of course, any service agent will give, but service costs money. Also, lacking any knowledge at all of the workings of the machine, the owner may allow a minor fault which could be adjusted in a minute to develop into a serious failure, necessitating a visit to the local garage and, possibly, a large repair bill.

The more you know about your machine, therefore, the better service you will get out of it, with a minimum of maintenance costs. You are less likely to damage vital working parts if you are aware of the dangers of letting the gearbox or rear axle run dry of oil and less likely to be stranded because the engine will not start, when perhaps the only fault is a fouled sparking plug which only needs taking out and cleaning, or replacing.

To achieve such a command over your Lambretta does not require extensive study of an unfamiliar subject. The workings of the machine can be described—and understood—in everyday language, except for the technical names given to the various components, and even these names can be picked up quickly. Those owners familiar with technicalities can skip this chapter if they wish; they will find all the information they require in Chapter VI.

HOW AN INTERNAL COMBUSTION ENGINE WORKS

Taking the various basic components in turn, probably the most important is the engine. An internal combustion engine, that is, an engine which burns its fuel inside it as opposed to, say a steam engine, where the water is heated outside the engine proper, consists essentially of a cylindrical shape, called a *piston*, free to move up and down inside a close-fitting tube, called a *cylinder*, suitably coupled to a shaft. This "coupling" consists of a rod, called a *connecting rod*, with the *little end* pivoted inside the piston by a stout pin, called the *gudgeon pin*, and the other end of the connecting rod, known as the *big end*, fitting over another pin, the *crank pin*, which in turn is fitted into a disc, the *crank web*, attached to a shaft, the *crankshaft*.

As Fig. 7 shows, up-and-down movement of the piston in the cylinder will cause the crankshaft to rotate in a given direction. Make sure that you understand this basic movement before reading on.

The Lambretta engine consists of just such a single-cylinder engine as this, shown in simplified form in Fig. 8. The crankshaft is a little different

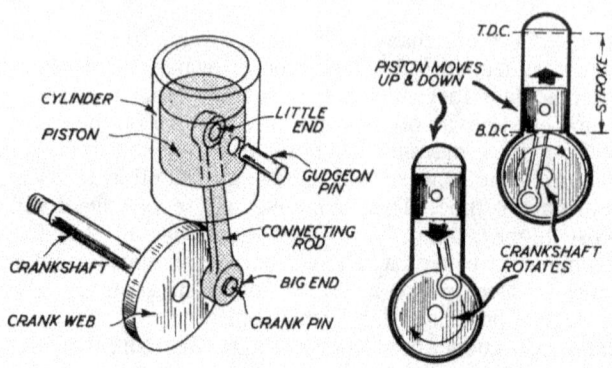

FIG. 7. THE BASIC PARTS OF A SINGLE-CYLINDER INTERNAL COMBUSTION ENGINE

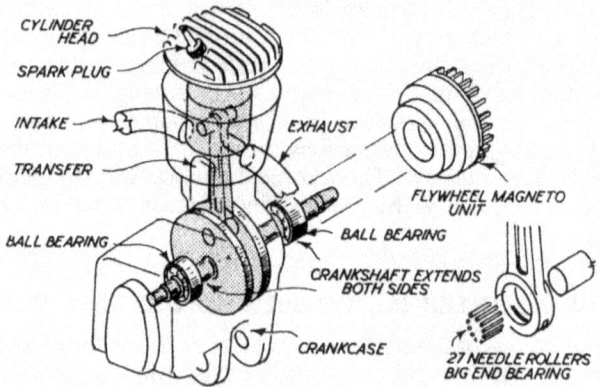

FIG. 8. SIMPLIFIED DRAWING OF THE LAMBRETTA ENGINE ASSEMBLY
On the 150 c.c. engine the big-end needles are assembled as an integral unit in a cage.

from the basic engine just described since its ends protrude on both sides of the crank web, one end providing driving power for the rear wheel and the other driving power for the *flywheel magneto* which is described later. It will also be noticed that the shaft is supported on *ball bearings* so that it can rotate easily with minimum resistance or friction. The big end bearing actually has thin, cylindrical-shaped *rollers* instead of steel balls, and is known technically as a needle-roller bearing. The little end bearing is a bronze sleeve or bush pressed into the connecting rod.

In the complete engine, the top of the cylinder is sealed off, with the *cylinder head* bolted down in place, and the crankshaft is enclosed in a cast-metal *crankcase*, in which the crankshaft bearings are fixed. The cylinder also has openings or *ports* cut in its walls, two opening direct to the outside—the *exhaust* and *intake ports* and a pair, called the *transfer ports*,

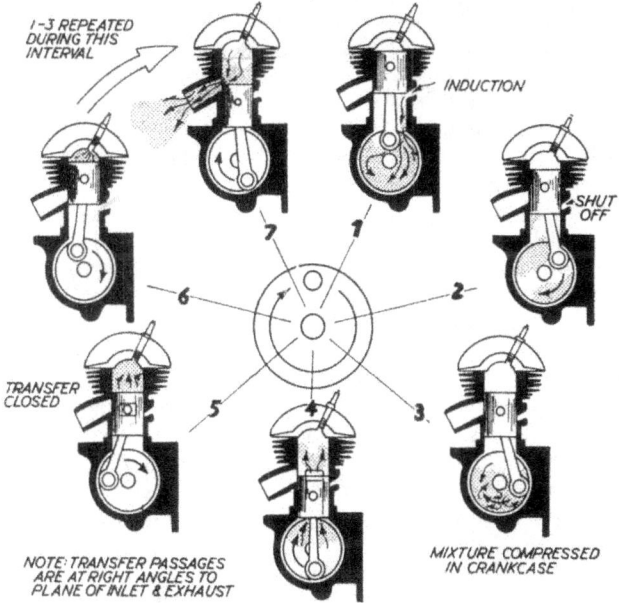

FIG. 9. THE TWO-STROKE CYCLE IN THE LAMBRETTA ENGINE
Timing of the gas flow is achieved by the size and location of the ports.

providing a gas passage down between a hollow section of the cylinder walls to the crankcase. These ports are shown clearly in Fig. 9 which illustrates the working of the engine. The transfer ports are in a plane at right angles to the exhaust and inlet ports.

The ports provide the means whereby the petrol is sucked into the engine, compressed, and eventually ejected or exhausted, after being burnt. To ignite the petrol at the proper instant a *spark plug* is screwed into the cylinder head. The basic elements of the spark plug are a central rod or electrode with a second electrode secured to the body of the plug and bent over so that it is almost touching the end of the first. At the requisite moment, as the engine turns over, i.e. the crankshaft revolves and the piston makes its up-and-down stroke, electricity from the *magneto* is supplied to the plug electrodes, sufficient in power to jump the gap between them, thus causing a spark. Magneto output is designed to give the hottest spark when the gap between the two plug electrodes is set to a predetermined figure, between 15 and 20 thousandths of an inch. The ends of the electrodes must also be electrically "clean" to give a good spark. Although there is quite a wide tolerance over which the plug will function, but not necessarily at its best, from the foregoing the significance of *spark plug gap adjustment* will be apparent.

The crankcase of the engine is a sealed unit. Thus, if the piston moves up the cylinder it is working like a pump and causing a suction pressure inside the crankcase. In Fig. 9 the working cycle of the engine is traced starting with the piston at the top of its stroke, called top dead centre, and usually abbreviated to T.D.C.

It will be seen that at T.D.C. (1) the piston has completely uncovered the *inlet* port, which is connected directly to the *carburettor*, the mechanical details of which we will ignore for the moment. As the intake port opens, through it a balanced, vapourized mixture of petrol and air is sucked from the carburettor into the crankcase and as the crankshaft continues to rotate the piston moves down the cylinder. Its first effect is to close off the intake port so that none of the fuel mixture already drawn in can escape (2).

As the piston travels still farther down the cylinder it begins to compress the fuel mixture in the crankcase (3) (*Note*. If the intake port were still open, fuel would be blown back through the carburettor) until, when approaching the bottom of its stroke (bottom dead centre, or B.D.C.) it uncovers the *transfer ports* (4) through which the mixture, now compressed into a relatively small volume, rushes from the crankcase to the top of the cylinder.

Starting its up stroke the piston now covers up the transfer port, thus sealing off the top of the cylinder (5), and continuing upwards compresses the mixture in the top of the cylinder. Just before reaching T.D.C. the spark plug is activated and ignites the compressed fuel mixture (6). Inertia carries the piston past T.D.C. until all the pressure of the expanding, burning fuel mixture exerts itself to push the piston downwards again. Having travelled far enough down for the maximum effective pressure of the burning fuel to be used up the piston uncovers the exhaust port which enables the burnt and now useless gases to escape from the cylinder (7).

If the diagrams are studied carefully it will be seen that although described separately above for clarity, certain things happen simultaneously. Thus at stage (6), where the mixture is on the point of being ignited the intake port is open, drawing in fuel as in stage (1). The whole cycle of operation—drawing in fuel mixture, pumping it from the crankcase to the top of the cylinder, igniting it, expanding it to produce power to drive the piston and exhausting the burnt gases—is completed in one "up" and one "down" stroke of the piston, which is why this type of engine is known as a two-stroke type. Once started, the operation of the engine will be continuous so long as fuel is fed to the intake port from the carburettor and a spark from the spark plug is fired automatically at the right time by the rotation of the crankshaft. The actual *timing* of the various phases of the cycle is determined by the position and size of the cylinder ports, and is a fixed feature of the engine design. The efficiency of the engine is also related to this port timing, together with the efficiency of the crankcase as a pump, the compression ratio achieved in the top of the

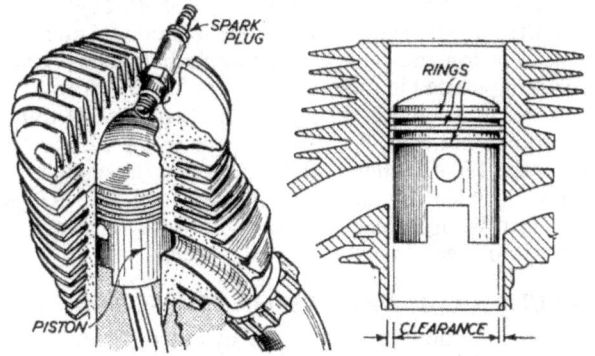

FIG. 10. SPRING-STEEL RINGS FITTED IN GROOVES ON THE PISTON FORM A GAS SEAL WITH THE CYLINDER WALL

The 125 c.c. engine has two rings, the 150 c.c. engine three.

cylinder on the up stroke, the diameter or bore of the cylinder, the length of stroke, and a number of other detail features.

Why the mixture is fired before T.D.C. is explained by the fact that there is a certain time lag between the spark jumping the gap between the plug electrodes and the effective expansion of the ignited mixture. In the Lambretta engine the actual timing is 26 degrees before T.D.C., i.e. the crankshaft has to rotate a further 26 degrees before the piston reaches T.D.C. Spark timing is also a function of engine speed and the faster the engine the earlier or more advanced should the spark occur. This is taken care of automatically on late models by a device coupled to the magneto unit which "advances" the spark, or mixture firing, point as engine speed increases. With ignition fixed, as on earlier models, it is set for the best high-speed timing.

It may also not be clear why the mixture has to be compressed in the top of the cylinder before it is ignited. This is largely because if the mixture is compressed it fires much more readily at a lower temperature and with more power. Thus the compression ratio of an engine is designed to give maximum performance from a given fuel. The higher the compression ratio the more one can get out of the fuel, although there are obvious practical limits. Also, to use a very high compression ratio special fuels are required. Ordinary fuels would ignite themselves through the heat generated by compression before the plug fired, giving the effect of excessively-advanced ignition, with uneven running and loss of power. The compression ratio of the Lambretta engine is designed for ordinary fuels and no advantage is to be gained in using higher octane premium petrols; in fact, performance may well be reduced.

A mechanical feature of importance is that since the piston is a pump it must be a good seal in the cylinder. If it were not, then much of the power of the expanding gases would be lost through leakage past the piston on the "down" stroke. To obtain a good seal and to reduce the friction between piston and cylinder to a minimum (which otherwise would mean power being wasted in moving the piston up and down) the piston is fitted with *rings*. The Lambretta piston has two rings of tough, springy steel set in grooves cut into the piston proper in the 125 c.c. engine, and three rings on the 150 c.c. engine, these rings bearing against the walls of the cylinder to provide the necessary gas seal, Fig. 10. Rings that seal badly, e.g. due to being broken or to a cylinder bore being worn out of true, must inevitably lead to loss of engine power.

MECHANICAL DETAILS OF THE LAMBRETTA

Mounted on the Lambretta frame, the cylinder of the engine is substantially vertical with the crankshaft at right angles to the frame. On the left side of the engine, on the left-hand crankshaft, is fitted the flywheel magneto, which also incorporates the cooling fan, Figs. 11*a* and 11*b*. It will be appreciated that the cylinder of the engine will get quite hot, so to prevent over-heating some form of cooling must be adopted. Air-cooling is more or less standard practice with small two-stroke vehicle engines, the outer surface of the cylinder being shaped in the form of fins to increase the effective area from which heat can be dissipated. Air blowing past these fins then helps maintain the cylinder at an even working temperature.

Adequate cooling thus relies on a moving stream of air flowing around the cylinder which, in the Lambretta, is achieved on all the later models (*see* Chapter I) by forced draught from a fan. The cylinder is shrouded with metal covers, and cooling air from the fan is blown around between the insides of these covers and the finned cylinder. Since the fan rotates at engine speed, the cooling air-flow is also matched to engine speed and is not dependent on forward motion of the vehicle, as in many air-cooled vehicle engines. The engine covers do not have to be detached to remove the spark plug which protrudes at an angle, on the left-hand side on 125 c.c. C and D models and on the right-hand side on all 150 c.c. engines and forced draught cooled versions, *i.e.* L models.

The Magneto. The magneto which supplies the spark to the plug is contained within the flywheel, the cooling air-fan blades being cast in as

Fig. 11 (a). All 150 c.c. Engines (and 125 c.c. L Models) have Forced Draught Cooling

Air is drawn in and circulated around the cylinder, the cooling rate thus being dependent on engine speed, not actual forward speed.

Fig. 11 (b). Access to the Contact Breaker for Checking is by Removing the Flywheel Cover and Hub

Take care not to lose the conical locking washers under the three cover screws.

an integral part of the flywheel rim. The purpose of the flywheel is to smooth out the running of the engine, carrying the piston on its "up" stroke and over T.D.C. by virtue of its inertia, on the same principle that if you apply spin to a toy top or gyroscope it will go on spinning when released.

The principle of operation of the magneto is a little complicated and need not be studied in detail at this stage; it is fully described in Chapter VI. It is sufficient to appreciate that production of a spark across the plug electrodes is dependent on a *contact breaker* unit consisting of one fixed and one moving point (contact) connected to the electrical circuit. When these points open, or *break*, they allow a sudden surge of high-voltage

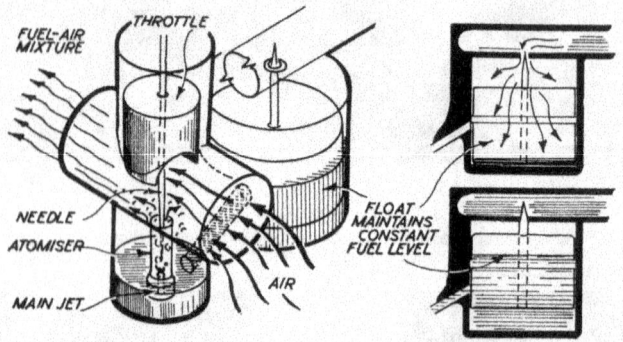

Fig. 12. A Simplified Drawing of the Carburettor, illustrating its Action

Fuel fed to the float chamber first passes through a filter. Suction from the engine atomizes the fuel and draws it into the crankcase. (*See* Figs. 56 and 57 for further drawings of the carburettor.)

electricity to pass through the lead connected to the spark plug. These points are revealed by removing the cover plate and are thus accessible for adjustment. Adjustment is dealt with in Chapters IV, VI, Section 10, and VII, but it is an item which should require only occasional attention.

The Carburettor. The speed of the engine is controlled by the amount of fuel mixture fed to it from the carburettor. Thus the carburettor is a device for mixing neat petrol with air, which has been sucked into the carburettor by the same suction pressure which draws the mixture into the engine.

The carburettor is mounted directly on the intake port on the right-hand side and slightly to the rear of the cylinder. Its operation can be studied in conjunction with the simplified diagram of its parts, Fig. 12. Fuel from the tank flows into a bowl attached to the far end of the carburettor, not shown in this sketch but clearly shown in Fig. 56, and thence up through a filter into the tubular passage above the float chamber. Here it is free to flow down through a small hole into the float chamber until the hollow float itself rises to such a height that the needle attached to it seals off this hole. Thus the function of the float is to maintain a constant level of fuel in the float chamber.

This fuel is tapped off into another small chamber in the left hand vertical extension of the carburettor. Exit from this chamber is through a "sized" jet opening, feeding into a perforated tube called an atomizer. The rate of flow through the atomizer is also controlled by upward and downward movement of a needle.

The needle is mounted in a throttle slide which also moves up and down and in so doing alters the extent of the air passage through the carburettor. Movement of the slide upwards allows a greater volume of air to flow through the carburettor and draws up more fuel-air mixture from the atomizer, thus increasing the *amount* of fuel-air mixture fed to the engine and making it run faster. Conversely, closing the slide, i.e. lowering it, reduces the volume of fuel-air mixture and so slows the engine. On the final carburettor there is also a small pilot air jet which when the slide is fully closed, supplies sufficient air to provide a mixture for "idling," i.e. engine running with the throttle fully closed. There are also two separate adjustment screws: one to adjust the "closed" position of the throttle slide so that the engine will continue to run without cutting out completely; and the other to adjust the mixture strength, i.e. the proportion of air to fuel, for smooth idling.

Another item also has to be added to assist in starting when the engine is cold, otherwise the mixture as drawn in would be too weak to fire properly before the cylinder had warmed up. On all the 125 c.c. engines this starting mixture device consists of an air slide which is depressed by hand for starting. On 150 c.c. engines the carburettor has a definite choke unit, similar to a car-engine carburettor, again operated manually. It is important, therefore, that the air slide or choke be returned to its normal "off" position once the engine has started and warmed up, otherwise the engine will continue to run on an excessively rich mixture, the air slide or choke being devices merely to alter the mixture and give a much higher proportion of petrol to air.

The Drive. Connexion between the engine shaft and rear wheel is by means of a shaft and gears, as shown in the very much simplified diagram Fig. 13. In actual fact, at the crankshaft end, for reasons which will be described later, there are very many more gears involved than the single pair shown. The shaft itself is made of extremely tough but flexible steel which enables it to absorb twisting loads. Thus, the coupling between engine and rear wheel has a certain amount of flexibility to enable it to absorb shocks, such as are given by a sudden acceleration of the engine, or when sharp braking is applied to the rear wheel with the engine driving hard. In this respect it is more foolproof than a chain drive normally associated with motor cycles, and quieter in operation. It is also quite clean since the whole of the transmission and gearing is fully enclosed in a metal casing protruding from, and bolting to, the rear face of the engine.

Such a directly-coupled drive as shown would, of course, be impracticable since the engine could not turn without at the same time driving the

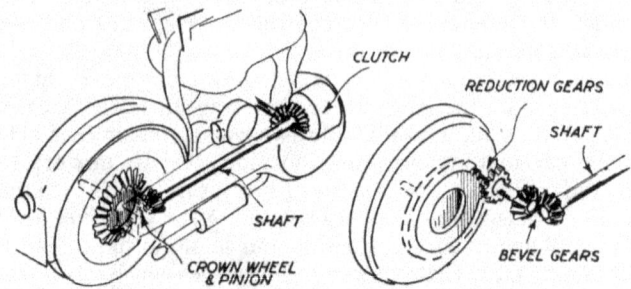

FIG. 13. SHOWING HOW THE ENGINE CRANKSHAFT IS LINKED TO THE REAR WHEEL BY A SHAFT DRIVE AND BEVEL GEARS

The sketch on the right shows the earlier system (C and LC models) in which the final drive is via reduction gears. Compare the left-hand sketch with Fig. 48 (b).

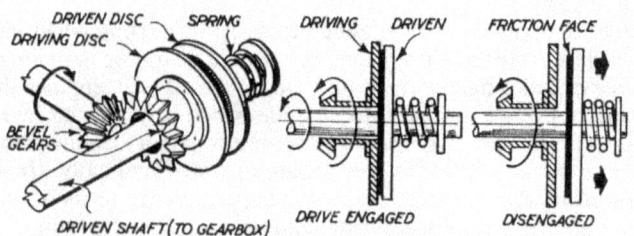

FIG. 14. SIMPLIFIED DRAWING OF THE PRINCIPLE OF CLUTCH ACTION

The Lambretta clutch actually has three driven plates and four driving plates (see Fig. 43).

rear wheel. Thus there would be no "stop" condition where the engine could be run, e.g. for starting, with the rear wheel remaining stationary. Thus some means of disconnecting the engine, at will, from the drive shaft has to be incorporated.

The Clutch. The mechanism which performs this function is the *clutch* which, again in much simplified form, is illustrated in Fig. 14. Here it will be seen that the engine drives only a short length of hollow shaft, the main transmission shaft running through the centre of this driven shaft and not being connected to it. Separate discs are fitted to both shafts, the inner face of one disc being lined with a material with high frictional qualities. As assembled, the two discs are pressed tightly together by means of a powerful spring. Thus, in this condition, the shaft driven by the engine and the transmission shaft to the rear wheel are effectively locked together and equivalent to a solid drive.

If the two discs are pulled apart, however, the engine will drive the one disc on the directly-coupled shaft but the transmission shaft will be quite free and so will not revolve. This separation is brought about by pulling the clutch lever on the left-hand handlebar. By *gradually* letting the clutch lever out again the two discs are brought together, slipping when they first contact, but with increasing "grip" as they come progressively closer until finally, with the clutch lever fully released, they are effectively locked solid.

Operation of the clutch is no more intricate than that. Once the principle is appreciated it will be understood that letting the clutch "out" slowly, i.e. letting the clutch *plates* come *together* gradually, will result in an even, progressive take-up of the drive. Letting the clutch out rapidly will suddenly connect the two shafts, where previously they were free from each other, when the suddenly applied load will make the machine jerk forward and probably stop or stall the engine. Whenever the clutch is operated, the engine is disconnected from the rear wheel, and thus no longer driving the machine. At intermediate clutch positions, engine and transmission shaft are connected but with a certain amount of "slip" or loss of a connecting link between them. While this is an advantage, in fact a necessity, for smooth starting from a standstill, slip increases the wear on the friction lining of the clutch. Conversely, a worn clutch, i.e. where the friction lining has been worn right down, may not provide a proper coupling even when the clutch is fully released. This invariably calls for replacement of the lining. On the other hand, a clutch that will not disengage the engine nearly always means that there is not enough movement to part the two discs sufficiently. This can be overcome by adjusting the length of the clutch cable. The Lambretta clutch actually consists of four steel driving discs, driven direct from the engine, set alternately with three driven plates, also of steel but faced with rubber-compound friction material on each side. The driven plates are keyed into a bell-shaped housing driven directly by the crankshaft, and the three driven discs key on to a splined collar locked on the driven shaft. The clutch is fully detailed in Chapter VI, Section 6 (*see also* Fig. 43).

Even with a clutch added, the transmission system is still not flexible enough for all driving conditions. Engine speed, for example, is limited to about 5,000 r.p.m. maximum, and even if it were made to go faster it would develop increasingly *less* power, because it is a characteristic of internal combustion engines that they develop a maximum power at a certain speed with a *decrease* in power output if run faster than this "peak" speed. The reason for this is quite simple. The efficiency of a two-stroke engine tends to increase with increasing speed (r.p.m.), up to a limit governed by the "timing" as decided by the porting arrangement, etc., and other factors. But with increasing speed comes increased internal friction, which means proportionately more power is used up in just keeping the engine going. There comes a point where these internal losses become increasingly greater and so beyond this point more and more power is being wasted in overcoming internal friction and the useful power output begins to fall off.

If the engine were coupled through the clutch shaft (and thence to the rear wheel) in such a drive ratio that would give it the required cruising speed of 35 m.p.h. with maximum fuel economy (100 to 120 m.p.g.) it would leave a nice reserve of power before the engine would "peak" to achieve a top speed of 45 m.p.h. or so. But it means that the engine would be running very slowly with the machine doing, say 5 to 10 m.p.h. Two-stroke engines do not run happily under load at low speeds, nor does any internal-combustion engine designed for fairly high maximum r.p.m. develop a great deal of power at low r.p.m. Thus the engine would tend to "snatch" and run jerkily. In fact in top gear the Lambretta will not run satisfactorily below 20 m.p.h. Also starting from a standstill would be very difficult. The engine would have to be revved right up and the clutch "slipped" extensively to get away, if such a get-away could be achieved at all.

The ideal arrangement for starting is a much reduced drive ratio between engine and rear wheel so that now the maximum power of the engine can be realized at a very much lower road speed for good starting and good initial acceleration. The gap between the two drive ratios required is large enough to warrant an intermediate ratio, so that best performance is realized with three distinct gear ratios available, as required.

The Gearbox. The mechanical operation of the gearbox in simple form is shown in Fig. 15. The transmission shaft of the previous examples is split into two parts, a main shaft which is driven by the engine, through the clutch, and a layshaft parallel to it. The rear-drive shaft is in line with the main shaft, but not coupled to it.

On the main shaft is a gear free to slide along the length of the shaft. There is also a similar gear, also free to slide, on the layshaft, these two gears being so made that they are actually locked together in respect of sideways movement. In other words, if one moves on its shaft the other travels with it on its shaft.

At the clutch end of the layshaft is a gear free to idle on the layshaft and mating with a smaller gear fixed to the main shaft. At the other end, the layshaft and rear transmission shaft are connected by a pair of gears secured to their respective shafts.

Now in the "neutral" gear position the mainshaft gear A is driving the layshaft gear *B*, but since *B* is free on the layshaft, the layshaft does not turn. This is also true because the pair of gears *C* and *D*, although in mesh with each other, are also on "free", or plain, lengths of their respective shafts.

Moving the gear selector to "first" then has the effect of moving gear *D* on the layshaft against gear *B* on the same shaft. Dogs on gear *D* engage in the face of gear *B* so that these two gears are now effectively coupled

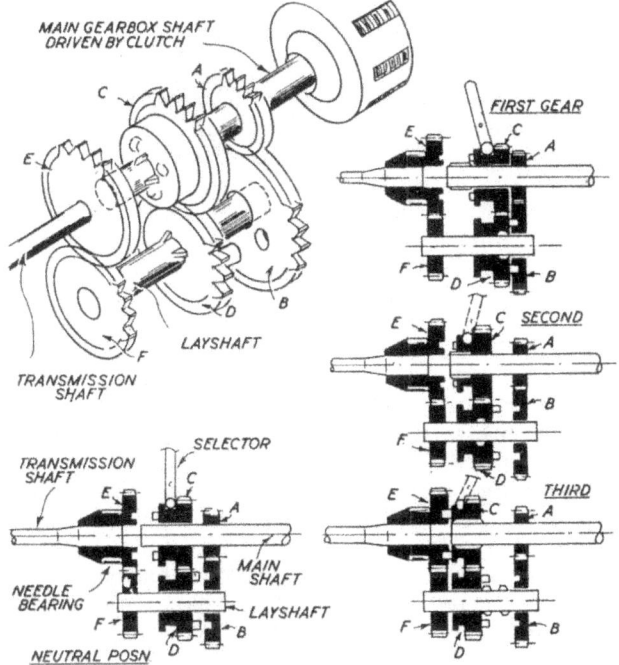

Fig. 15. The Lambretta Gearbox Simplified, but with all Relevant Parts Shown

Gear change is by shifting the gear pair *C* and *D*. Gears *A* and *B* are always in mesh with each other; also gears *E* and *F*.

together. Gear *C* has also moved along the main shaft with gear *D*, but is still on a free length of shaft and thus does not contribute anything. Gear *D* in moving along the layshaft has, however, run on to a splined section of the shaft and so is locked to the shaft. Hence the layshaft is driven by gear *A* through *B*, connected to the shaft by being locked to *D*, and the gears *F* and *E* transmit this drive to the transmission shaft. Since gear *B* is larger than gear *A* the drive speed is therefore considerably lower than the engine speed.

Moving to second gear, the gear pair C and D are slid back along their respective shafts and both lock on to a splined length on each shaft at this point. Hence they provide a coupling between the shafts (with a different gear ratio this time), once again transmitting drive to the transmission shaft, but at a somewhat higher gear ratio. Gear A is still driving gear B it will be noticed, but B is merely idling on the layshaft.

In top gear position, gear C is pushed right up against gear E and, like D engaging B in first gear, locks on to it by means of specially-shaped dogs. Gear D, which has moved with C, has now run on to a plain length of the layshaft and so is just idling. The drive, in fact, is now coupled straight through from the clutch end of the main shaft to the rear transmission shaft. The layshaft is idling with the transmission shaft. Because gears E and F are always in mesh, the layshaft is, in fact, always rotating at the same speed ratio with the transmission shaft, irrespective of which gear is involved.

How gear changing is effected may appear a little complicated at first but it is readily mastered with a little study. It is necessary to understand the function and working of the gearbox should it be necessary to dismantle it at any time.

Kick-starter. For the purpose of starting the engine all Lambretta models except the 125 c.c. LDA machines are provided with a conventional kick-starter. This is nothing more than a foot-operated pedal which, when depressed, engages a quadrant-shaped gear with a pinion connected to the engine shaft (*see* Chapter VI, Section 5). Further depression of the kick-starter lever then spins this pinion and rotates the engine. As soon as the engine is turned over the pumping action of the crankcase is effective in sucking in fuel and the magneto is activated for the production of a spark at the sparking plug. The kick-starter is retained on the 150 c.c. Model LDA, which has an electric starter motor operated by a lever control on the handlebars (*see* Chapter VI, Section 14).

Brakes. The Lambretta brakes follow conventional practice and consist of pivoted shoes which are expanded outwards, by movement of the brake lever, to press friction faces against the inner surface of a metal drum attached to the wheel. The necessary mechanical movement for operating the rear brake is provided by a foot pedal actuating a cable or rod linkage to the rear wheel. (The rod system is applicable only to C and LC models and early 125 c.c. D and LD models.) The front brake shoes are expanded by means of a cable operated by a pull lever on the right-hand handlebar. Fig. 16 illustrates the main features of the system diagrammatically. Brake adjustment consists largely of taking up "slack" in the linkage, or cable, to compensate for wear on the linings, replacement shoes being required when the lining has worn to the extent where it it no longer effective (*see* Chapter IV).

PARTS OF THE LAMBRETTA 25

Suspension. The suspension of the Lambretta is most effective, resulting in a very smooth ride. For the rear suspension on D and LD models, engine, gearbox, transmission, and rear wheel together form an integral unit swinging on a strong pivot incorporated in the frame of the machine.

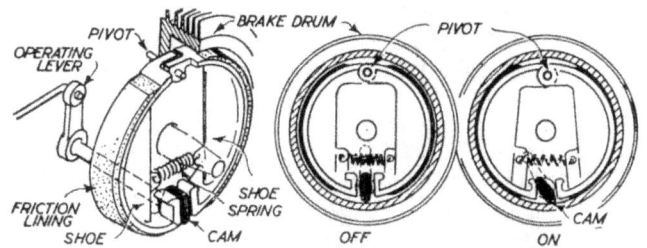

FIG. 16. OPERATING PRINCIPLE OF THE FRONT AND REAR BRAKES

The brake lever is directly connected to a cam and, when turned, expands the shoes so that their friction linings rub against the inside of the brake drum.

To take up the shocks when the back wheel is travelling over rough surfaces a torsion bar is fitted underneath the engine across the machine and connected to the engine by means of a stout link.

The torsion bar itself is simply a rod of special steel readily capable

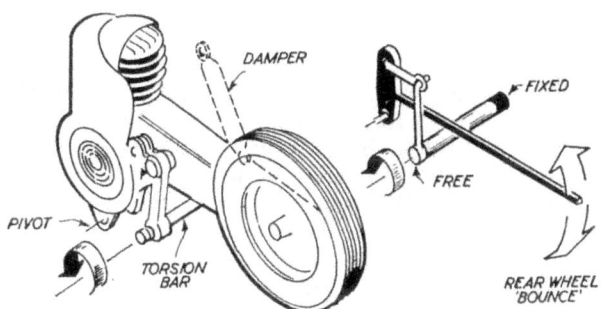

FIG. 17. DIAGRAM OF THE TORSION-BAR REAR SUSPENSION

Up and down movement is transferred as a "twist" to the torsion bar.

of absorbing twisting (i.e. torsion) loads; the more it is twisted the more resistant it becomes. Thus, as Fig. 17 shows, this has the effect of providing an effective spring action for the rear wheel, complete with engine unit. The ride is further improved by fitting a shock absorber between the transmission casing and the main frame, the attachment of such a damper being a standard feature of all the 150 c.c. engine machines. The mechanics of the torsion bar suspension are dealt with in detail in Chapter VI, Section 7.

Front wheel suspension is more conventional, Fig. 18. The front wheel itself is mounted with a trailing link on each side of it, free to move through a fairly generous arc. Thus when the wheel travels over a rough surface the trailing links tend to float up and down, giving a corresponding movement to levers to which they are rigidly connected. The free ends of these levers bear against coil springs located in the front forks themselves

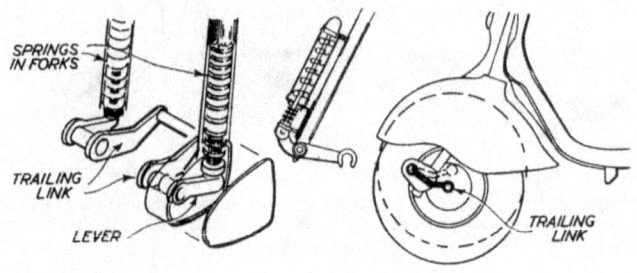

FIG. 18. THE FRONT SUSPENSION IS SPRUNG BY MEANS OF COIL SPRINGS HOUSED IN THE HOLLOW FORKS, OPERATED BY A LEVER SYSTEM

The smaller sketch illustrates the C and LC model suspension. Here the coil springs are housed outside the forks.

which therefore take up and dampen out the shocks. Rubber pads at the extreme bottom ends of the forks absorb any return movement shocks. The suspension elements are housed in the oval-shaped grease-tight casings protruding from the front forks on either side of the wheel.

On the C and LC models, the front suspension operates on a somewhat different principle. The main compression spring (there is one on each side) is housed in a cylinder attached to the front of the forks and is actuated by a tie rod linked to a pivoted lever on which the wheel is mounted. Upward movement of the wheel pulls the tie rod downward to compress the spring. Another smaller spring fitted outside the main-spring housing damps the return action of the main-spring. This different action is illustrated in the smaller diagram.

CHAPTER III

HANDLING THE LAMBRETTA

THE STARTING POINT for a new driver is to mount the Lambretta on its stand. The stand is spring loaded to tuck up underneath the engine. It can be trapped by a foot and the machine pulled backwards up on to its stand by grasping the seat. On later models a spur extension on the left-hand side of the stand enables the stand to be lowered by the foot, further foot pressure pulling the machine up to its standing position, as above. In all cases stand by the left side of the machine for this operation.

The stand supports the Lambretta at roughly its normal balance point, so that it can be tipped slightly either way. This is done deliberately so that either wheel can be raised clear of the ground if required, e.g. for a wheel change. The stand is adequate support provided it is let down over substantially level, hard surfaces. It will sink in, and possibly let the machine tip over, on soft ground; a point to be remembered. It is considered unwise for the rider to sit on the machine when it is mounted on its stand since this could result in strain and deformation of the fitting.

THE LAMBRETTA CONTROLS

The disposition and function of the various controls has been described in the previous chapter. They are, however, again shown collectively in Figs. 19*a* and 19*b*. All the main controls, with the exception of the rear wheel brake, are within ready reach of either hand without having to take the hands off the handlebar grips. The gear change on the left-hand side, Fig. 20, and the throttle (speed control) on the right-hand side, Fig. 21, are operated by twisting the grips themselves, a method which is easy to master. The gear change should not really be operated with the machine stationary and the engine stopped, although getting the "feel" of changing into first gear by way of practice is permissible. Do not, however, try to force the gear change into second or third if it will not go easily.

Before attempting to ride the machine the beginner should experiment in starting the engine. Starting procedure is extremely straightforward and if followed *correctly* will normally give almost instantaneous results. Lacking any initial experience, however, one can do the silliest things without realizing it. The common fault with novices is to persist in kicking away at the starter in a sort of furious desperation when it is pretty obvious that there is something wrong. The engine should start within half a dozen kicks, provided the correct technique is followed, and normally in

Fig. 19 (a). All Driving Controls are Located on the Handlebars, with the Exception of the Foot Brake. Model Shown is a 150 c.c. LD

Carburettor controls are under the tank on 125 c.c. models and the right-hand side panel has an access panel to reach them.

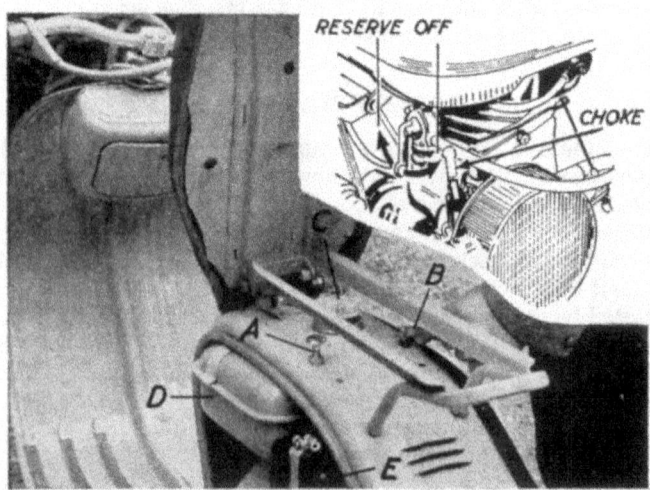

Fig. 19 (b). Filler Cap C is Situated above the Rear Mudguard on all Models

In this version the driver's and pillion seats are combined as one and lift up. Choke A and petrol tap B have same position on all 150 c.c. LD models. Left-hand side panel is removed to show tank D and the battery E which is carried by machines with parking lights. The small drawing shows position of petrol tap and choke on the 150 c.c. D models.

less. If it does not, then further kicking over may draw in excess mixture, "wet" the plug, and prevent its firing.

To start with the engine cold it is necessary to use the choke or starter control. If the machine has been standing idle for several days, or

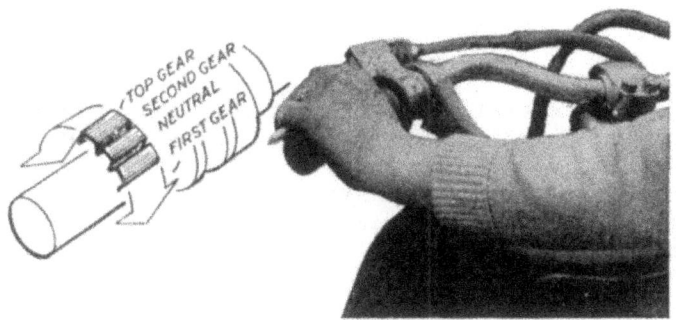

Fig. 20. The Clutch Lever is Mounted on the Gear-change Twist Grip and so Rotates with it

The clutch must always be operated to change gear with engine running, but should be released completely when running in gear

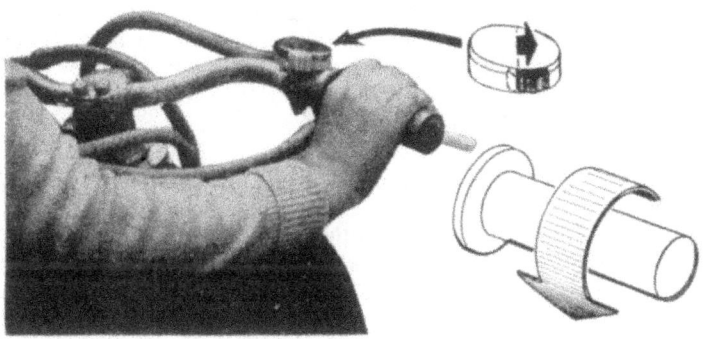

Fig. 21. Rotate Throttle Twist-grip Towards you to Increase Engine Speed

Grip is spring-loaded to return to the closed position if released. Engine only stops if switch is pushed to right as far as it will go; it is easily reached by thumb without taking the hand off the grip.

over-night in cold weather, first operate the kick-starter vigorously two or three times to free the oil. Then proceed as for a normal "cold" start.

All 125 c.c. models have an airslide fitted to the carburettor in place of a choke, controlled by a small pedal-type lever protruding from the top of the unit. This is lifted to its fullest extent for starting. All 125 c.c. models also have a "tickler" on the top of the carburettor float chamber in the form of a simple button. When this is depressed it pushes down the float, thus enabling the float chamber to fill with fuel. As soon as the float chamber is full, excess fuel escapes through a small hole near the top and the appearance of wetness on the side of the float chamber is an indication that the fuel is overflowing and no further "tickler" manipulation is necessary. On the 125 c.c. L-type models, access to the carburettor for manipulating the starting controls is through a small hinged panel on the right-hand side fairing panel.

On all 150 c.c. models the carburettors have a choke control. In the Model D machines the choke lever emerges from the top of the carburettor in the form of a hinged lever. When this lever is lifted up to its fullest extent the choke is in the starting position. On LD models the choke is extended to emerge from the top of the rear mudguard immediately behind the driver's seat on the left-hand side (or under the combined driver-passenger seat, which lifts up). It terminates in a knob and the choke is actuated by pulling this knob up to its fullest extent. Rotating it half a turn then locks it in the fully-choked position for starting.

The petrol tap is located on top of the tank roughly opposite the choke on 150 LD models and immediately underneath the tank on the right-hand side on D models (*see* Fig. 19*b*). This tap (marked *B*) should be turned to the "on" position. Two or three smooth but powerful downstrokes on the kick-starter should then get the engine running, bearing in mind that the faster the engine is turned over the more readily it should start. If nothing happens, then the throttle should be held open about a quarter of a turn and the process repeated. Normally, however, with the choke fully out, the throttle should be left closed.

Starting Troubles. Close the choke control as soon as the engine is running properly. The new owner is likely to overlook this in his excitement at getting away with the result that the engine will be running on an excessively rich mixture and will lack pulling power. If the engine has *not* started in the two separate attempts just described, then it is again advisable to close the choke, open the throttle half way, or slightly more, and try kicking over again. Nearly always the cause of poor starting is excessive use of the choke, especially in warm weather, resulting in the inside of the cylinder and the plug becoming saturated with liquid fuel so that no spark is possible. Provided this condition is not too bad it may be possible to relieve it by shutting off the choke, opening the throttle wide and kicking over vigorously. If things have gone too far for this method to work, then the best thing to do is to take out the plug and dry it off or replace it with another one. Before replacing, kick the engine over vigorously half a dozen times to blow some of the excess mixture out of the top of the cylinder, holding the ignition switch in the cut-off position as a precaution.

If the plug is taken out, then you can double-check for possible trouble by replacing the high-tension lead and holding the plug *by the insulated lead* in contact with the side of the engine. Operate the kick-starter, which you can now do by hand, if you find it easier, and see that the plug is sparking properly before you put it back. If you still get negative results then you can check if the magneto is providing a spark by disconnecting the high-tension lead from the plug and holding the lug about $\frac{3}{16}$ to $\frac{1}{4}$ inch away from the engine or magneto case, *again grasping the insulated portion of the lead* (see Fig. 28a). Operate the kick-starter again when you should get a spark from the end of the lead. That then locates the ignition failure in the plug itself.

The majority of starting, or running, troubles with two-stroke engines running on petroil mixtures are invariably traceable to the sparking plug and so an essential requirement is to know how to remove the plug; simply unscrew it with the standard spanner supplied with the machine's tool kit. As a wise precaution, always carry a new or clean plug as a spare.

Other starting troubles, far less likely than plug trouble, may be caused by malfunctioning of the carburettor or magneto and may be traced via the trouble-shooting charts given in Chapter V. There is also, of course, the very obvious fault of no petrol in the tank, or the spark plug lead being accidentally disconnected. Lack of fuel may also be responsible for the engine stopping after a short run. There may be enough fuel standing in the carburettor to get the engine running, then after a little while it cuts out, simply because the petrol tap is in the "off" position.

When the engine is reasonably warm—any time within an hour or so of a previous run on a warm day, for instance—no choke should be necessary for starting. Opening up the throttle about one eighth and kicking over should be adequate. With your initial practice runs, therefore, remember that once you have started and run your engine, subsequent re-starts require only a partially-opened throttle before kicking over.

Apart from the knack of getting the engine running with the minimum of fuss, some practice is also necessary to master kick-starting from a sitting position on the machine. Lower the machine off its stand for this, leaning to the left to support yourself, and the machine, with the left foot on the ground. Also get familiar with kick-starting the machine off its stand when standing to the right of it, holding it upright by grasping the handlebar grips. The sooner you master these techniques the sooner you will stop looking awkward and less like a complete novice.

It should, of course, be unnecessary to emphasize that all starts should be made with the gear control in the "neutral" position. It will be obvious if it is not. The machine will try to run forwards as you bear down on the kick-starter, if on the ground; or the rear wheel will start to spin, if the machine is on its stand.

Having mastered starting, the time to move off under power has arrived. The machine should be started up without the stand. Make sure that the stand is tucked up fully; it does not normally spring right up when the machine is rolled forward off the stand. Make sure also that you have a clear and *straight* run in front of you. It is that much more awkward for a beginner if there is a curve to negotiate immediately after getting under way. Also start well out from the side of the road or kerb to leave room for an involuntary weave in that direction.

Pull the clutch lever in to the full amount of its travel and *then* rotate the left-hand grip towards you. This puts the machine into first gear. Rotate the right-hand grip to open the throttle to about a quarter of its full travel, keep it there, and then gradually let off the clutch, but maintain a grip on the clutch lever. If the latter is accomplished smoothly the engine will "bite," gradually pulling the machine away from its standing start. A sudden jerk, with the engine stopping dead, means that you have let the clutch out too rapidly and/or you have not opened the throttle enough. A sudden jerk and away, with the engine still running, means you have opened the throttle too much. Practise altering the throttle adjustment slightly at the same time as you let out the clutch to give a smooth getaway.

If you want to stop, the simple rule is, pull both levers. Pulling back the clutch lever disengages the engine, so that even if you have accidentally revved it up to near maximum speed it will no longer be driving. Pulling the right-hand lever applies the front brake. So you come to a standstill. Put the gear change back to neutral *before* letting go of the clutch lever. If you want a break, just operate the ignition cut-out control with the right thumb to stop the engine.

Once you can get away respectably in first gear, remember to pull your feet in and put them on the floor-boards as soon as you are moving at a safe speed. The novice is apt to continue to trail both feet overboard on his first trips. There is plenty of time when you do stop to put a foot out at the appropriate side to keep the machine upright.

Gear Changing. Once you can get away satisfactorily, too, there is no need to stop in first gear. Accelerate by opening up the throttle until you have reached a reasonable speed, or the noise of the engine frightens you, then, simultaneously, close the throttle and pull the clutch fully. Then operate the gear change, rotating away from you two clicks to "second" position. Repeat the process after you have accelerated still more in this gear to change up into the third position or "top."

Faults at this stage will be obvious. A pronounced braking effect as you start to change gear will mean that you have closed the throttle before operating the clutch. If the engine revs up rapidly, you have operated the clutch before closing the throttle. You will also find that you can let out the clutch much more rapidly after each change than when pulling away from a standing start.

Changing down through the gears requires a slightly different procedure.

Operate the clutch, shift down one gear with a twist movement towards you, then let out the clutch again smoothly, at the same time *opening* the throttle. If you remember the action of the gearbox described in Chapter II you will see that for the same road speed in a lower gear, which means, simply, for the same rate of rotation of the back wheel, the *engine* must be going faster in the lower gear. So make this compensation by opening the throttle when letting out the clutch to engage the lower gear. The Lambretta gearbox is designed to compensate for such speed differences when gear changing, but help with the throttle is good driving practice.

Knowing when to change down is largely a matter of experience. For normal cruising over substantially level roads with no need to slow down for obstructions is top gear work. Coming to a hill the engine will tend to slow down and, if it shows signs of labouring (you will hear this in the form of a knocking or rattling sound, if it is allowed to persist) a change down to second gear is called for. Once able to accelerate away again you can go back into top gear as soon as you have picked up enough speed.

The general rule is that if the engine is obviously running laboured and "snatching" at the drive, or the machine will not speed up at once when the throttle is opened, then you should change down to a lower gear. This state of affairs is often experienced by the novice when changing *up*. Here this is either due to changing up too soon, i.e. at too low a road speed, or to accidentally changing from first into top, instead of second. The Lambretta will not drive satisfactorily in top gear below a road speed of 20 m.p.h.

Changing down into second gear is also a useful method of slowing down before coming to a corner. Once second gear has been engaged the throttle can be closed so that the engine acts as a brake, then opened up again once round the corner to accelerate away. Dropping down to a very low speed, such as walking pace, it will be necessary to change down to first gear to prevent the engine from "snatching."

ON THE HIGHWAY

The gears are there for a purpose and the good driver uses them properly so that the engine is always running at an efficient speed. Top-gear driving throughout is not good practice on a run which demands slowing down and accelerating away at frequent intervals. When the engine is labouring it is working less efficiently and imposing extra strain on the bearings and transmission. Two-stroke engines are generally happiest when they are running fairly fast and made to work quite hard.

Running-in. A brand new machine, however, needs careful "running-in," just like a motor car. The same applies to a machine just refitted with a replacement engine. This is because the moving parts are originally set up to be a little on the tight side so that they will wear down to really good running fits and so give maximum life and maximum performance from the engine.

Running in is not a critical or exacting process, especially with a two-stroke engine. It really means avoiding *excessive* engine speeds, i.e. not running the engine flat out for any lengthy period until the machine has completed some four to five hundred miles. It is more important to avoid "racing" the engine off load, i.e. in neutral gear, than when actually travelling in any gear. The following are recommended *maximum* speeds not to be exceeded in any gear with a brand new machine, or a new engine.

Under 100 *miles* (as registered on the mile counter). Do not exceed *one half* the full throttle opening on any gear.

100–300 *miles*. Do not hold at *full throttle* for more than a few seconds in any gear.

300–500 *miles*. Do not dwell extensively at full throttle unless the engine is obviously quite free.

After this you should be quite safe in revving up to maximum engine speed in any gear, equivalent approximately to: First, 20 m.p.h.; Second, 30 m.p.h.; Third, 45 m.p.h.

Maximum speed in third will vary somewhat with different machines, depending on small differences in detail design and on how they have been run-in. Most new machines will tend to remain a little stiff for the first 1,000 miles or so. Remembering that stiffness means internal friction it is easy to appreciate that the stiffer the engine the lower its power "peak"; and the greater the internal friction the hotter the engine will tend to get. If it gets too hot, moving parts may expand to the point where they "seize," which can damage the surfaces involved. This, however, is most unlikely to happen even to a brand new Lambretta engine driven hard. But excessive hard driving when the engine is new can reduce its useful life.

Cornering. The technique of cornering is the same as with any two-wheeled vehicle; machine and rider have to lean inwards on turns. This is because any object made to move in a circular path is subjected to a force tending to pull it outwards away from the circle. This is demonstrated by the very simple experiment of swinging a stone or weight tied to a length of string around in a circle. The stone or weight pulls outwards to keep the string taut. If the string were released the weight would fly outwards in a straight line.

This outward reaction, commonly referred to as centrifugal force, acts through the centre of weight or *centre of gravity* of the object. Thus in a two-wheeled vehicle cornering, the height of the centre of gravity has a marked bearing on the effect of centrifugal force. As will be seen in Fig. 22, the "overturning" effect of a high centre of gravity is greater than that of a low centre of gravity. For machines of the same weight making a similar radius of turn at the same speed the difference in the two overturning forces is the ratio of the heights of the two centres of gravity.

HANDLING THE LAMBRETTA 35

Leaning the machine inwards automatically corrects the overturning effect when cornering, since the weight of the machine is now displaced to one side of the point of support, i.e. the point of contact of the tyre and road surface, producing an opposite overturning force. The rider's sense

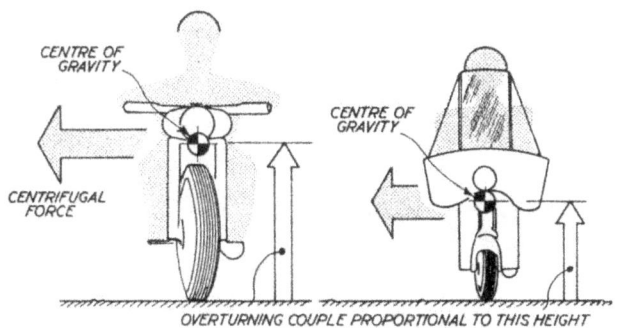

Fig. 22. Cornering Produces an Overturning Force on all Two-wheeled Vehicles

The lower the centre of gravity of the machine and rider the less this force.

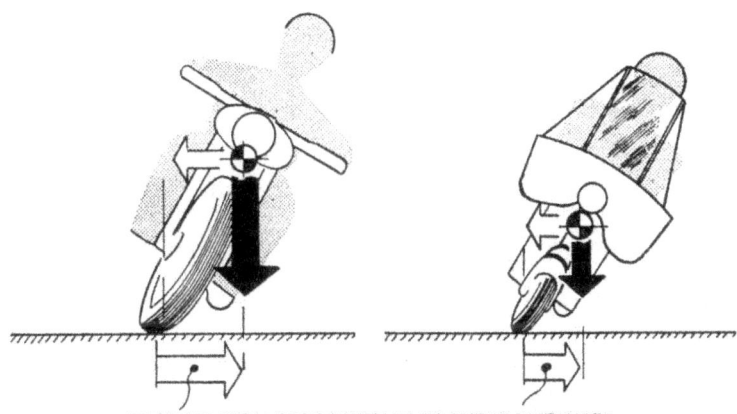

Fig. 23. Banking Inwards Produces an Opposite Overturning Force to Balance Centrifugal Force

The angle of bank required to compensate is independent of centre of gravity height. The faster the turn, or the smaller the radius, the greater the bank required.

of balance automatically adjusts the amount of "lean in," or bank, so that the two opposing overturning forces cancel each other out, Fig. 23.

Comparing again machines with high and low centres of gravity it is interesting to note that both require the *same* angle of bank for similar weight of machine, speed and turning radius. The low centre of gravity reduces the power of the "corrective" force as well as the original "overturning" force and the two cancel out at the same angle of bank. Thus, although the low centre of gravity of the Lambretta reduces the overturning force when cornering, to correct it needs a similar angle of bank as any other two-wheeled vehicle of the same weight.

The value of the overturning force also increases with speed, weight and decreasing turning radius. This means, quite simply, the faster you go into a turn, or the smaller the turning radius, the more centrifugal force

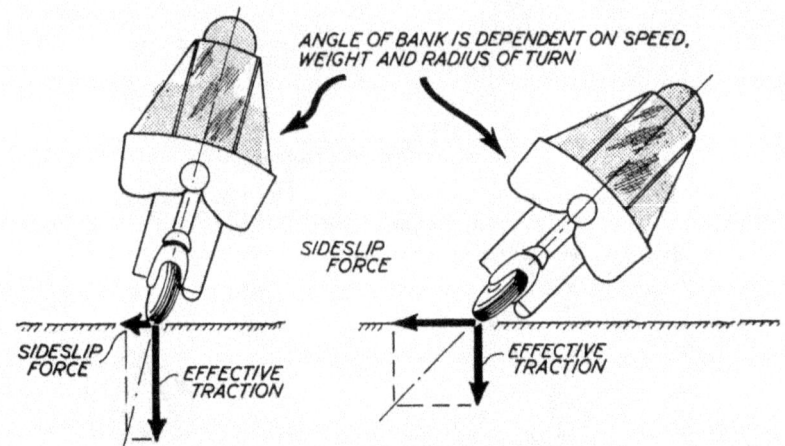

FIG. 24. THE ANGLE OF BANK REQUIRED TO ACHIEVE BALANCE DEPENDS ON SPEED, WEIGHT AND RADIUS OF TURN

Increasing the angle of bank decreases the effective grip of the tyres and increases the sideslipping force.

generated by the machine and the greater the inward bank required to maintain stability. The only other factor which then affects stability is the grip between the tyres and the road surface.

Whatever the angle of bank in a turn, the resultant force or pressure between tyre and road surface will be in line with the machine, Fig. 24. This resultant force will act effectively in two directions: a sideways force tending to skid the machine outwards away from the turn, and a downward force which determines the effective grip or traction between tyre and road. The sideways force is resisted by the grip of the tyre on the road and can become quite high, i.e. the angle of bank can be quite large, before the tyre will slip if the tyre is in good condition and the road surface is firm and dry.

Where the road surface is very slippery, however, quite a moderate angle of bank can result in slipping. Once the tyre does start to slip sideways it immediately increases the angle of bank and so makes things worse and the machine will tend to slide sideways from under the rider. This may happen far too quickly for the inexperienced rider to take any corrective action. It therefore pays to be cautious on slippery roads, going into corners more slowly and taking them wider so that very little bank is required. A *wet* road is not necessarily a slippery road, but traction is generally reduced and it pays to treat such conditions with caution. On wet or greasy roads, too, it is generally best to use the engine (closing the throttle) for slowing, but use *both* brakes simultaneously for quicker stopping.

Stopping. For all braking it is best practice to use both front and rear brakes simultaneously. This gives the most powerful braking effect with even wear on brake linings and tyres. The good driver, however, uses his brakes as little as possible; he avoids getting into situations where he has to stop suddenly, and he uses the *throttle* as the primary control. The engine, throttled back, is a most effective brake for slowing down in normal circumstances.

To stop completely, the throttle is closed by rotating the twist grip the fullest extent away from you, the clutch lever operated (clutch disengaged) as soon as the speed has fallen, and both brakes applied gently and simultaneously. Brake pressure can then be increased progressively, as required. Rotate the left-hand grip to neutral gear position before releasing the clutch and then operate the ignition cut-off to stop the engine. If the machine is not to be restarted right away, switch off the petrol by turning the tap to the position marked "C".

The main thing the novice has to learn is to relax when driving his machine. It is natural at first to grip the handlebars so tightly that the hands feel quite painful after a while. The correct grip is firm, but relaxed and unstrained. The same applies to the riding position. It should be comfortable, not strained forward. This will come with practice and at the same time such control movements as braking and gear changing will become instinctive.

If a slide develops on a slippery road surface the immediate action must be *to release the brake and clutch*. In other words. if a skid or slide develops, never apply the brakes in an attempt to correct because this will only make matters worse. Or if a slide develops on the application of brakes, release the brakes immediately. The correct action in a *back wheel slide* is to turn in the direction in which the wheel is slipping. A front wheel slide is rather more difficult to correct, but here the correct action is to open the throttle and straighten out by accelerating.

Small wheels provide greater stability than large wheels because the gyroscopic reaction is less and because the wheels are more readily turned to correct any deviation from the correct course. Gyroscopic action takes effect in the following manner. Movement of the handlebars displaces the spinning front wheel, acting like a gyroscope, and induces a force tending to produce an *opposite* bank which is required to stabilize the turn. Applying bank without turning the handlebars from the straight ahead position induces a force tending to turn the machine in the direction of the applied bank. Thus, leaning to one side or the other is essentially a *stable* movement whereas handlebar movement alone introduces an unstabilizing factor which must be corrected, e.g. by bank or leaning over.

CHAPTER IV

REGULAR MAINTENANCE

THE MOVING PARTS of the engine are lubricated internally by oil mixed with the petrol. This is done by filling the tank with a petrol-oil (petroil) mixture of the correct proportion: half a pint of lubricating oil for each gallon of petrol. For new engines, up to about 500 miles running, a slightly higher proportion of oil is recommended to make sure that adequate lubrication is maintained if the engine tends to run hotter than usual.

FUEL MIXTURE

The recommended proportion of oil to petrol should be adhered to strictly. Also the correct *grade* of oil should always be used, specified as SAE 30. The SAE number rating of oils is based on their viscosity or thickness. The higher the SAE number the thicker the oil, and *vice versa*. It is largely an arbitrary classification and is not necessarily a measure of the *quality* of the oil. Thus, it is a wise precaution to insist on using a known brand of oil of the appropriate grade (SAE 30), such as Castrol XL, Energol 30, Essolube 30, Mobiloil A, Shell SAE 30.

Commercial grade petrol is satisfactory. There is, in fact, no advantage at all to be gained in using premium grades in the Lambretta engine, nor with petrols containing special additives. Similarly, it is unnecessary to mix shots of upper-cylinder lubricant or similar additives with the fuel. The relatively high oil content of the correct petroil mixture will ensure adequate engine lubrication, provided the right grade of a good quality oil is always adhered to.

If an excess of oil is used in the mixture this will tend to soot up the inside of the engine and silencer, calling for early decarbonizing, without improving the engine lubrication. An excess of oil in the mixture will not, however, be harmful otherwise and up to twice the recommended proportion of oil can be used without affecting performance.

Too little oil in the mixture will reduce the lubricating effect to a dangerous level, resulting in high wear on the moving parts and eventually failure or seizure. The same effect will be present if the oil is of poor quality which breaks down under the running temperature of the engine, or the oil is too thin. Too thick an oil may not be so harmful but it will tend more readily to settle out of the petrol as a separate layer. Any marked departure from the recommended mixture will also affect the carburettor jet settings and so will not give such efficient running.

40 THE BOOK OF THE LAMBRETTA MOTOR-SCOOTER

Ideally the petrol and oil should be mixed in a separate can before pouring into the tank. A standard one gallon can will just take half a pint of oil with one gallon of petrol poured on top. If the can is turned end for end several times this will disperse the oil through the petrol and give a homogenuous mixture which can then be poured into the tank via a suitable funnel.

If it is more convenient to fill the tank direct—such as when pulling in at a filling station—one gallon of petrol should be put into the tank first

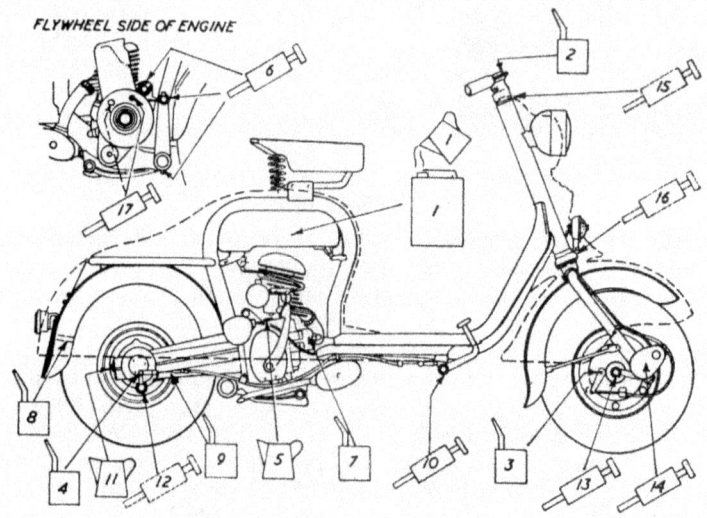

FIG. 25. LUBRICATION DIAGRAM FOR ALL LAMBRETTA MODELS
(Refer to Lubrication Table for complete details.) Oil-can or grease-gun points are defined.

and the half pint of oil poured on top. The filler cap should then be replaced on the tank and the machine shaken from side to side to ensure the oil mixing evenly.

With the increasing number of two-stroke engines using petroil mixtures many filling stations are equipped to dispense either ready-mixed petroil or to spray in the oil through a special nozzle so that it gives complete and instant mixing with the petrol in the tank. In such cases, of course, the mixture needs no further agitation.

Once mixed thoroughly there is normally no tendency for the heavier oil to separate out from the petrol, except possibly in extremely cold weather. If a machine has been left standing for several days in the cold with fuel in the tank, shake first to re-mix any oil which has tended to separate out, otherwise the initial mixture drawn into the engine may be excessively oily and foul up the plug.

REGULAR MAINTENANCE

LUBRICATION

The remaining parts of the machine require lubricating at regular intervals. There are two separate reservoirs of oil, one for the gearbox and one for the back axle, the remaining parts requiring attention being lubricated

Lubrication Table

When	Ref.	Part(s) to be Lubricated	Lubricant (and Remarks)
Weekly	1	Engine	Continuously lubricated by oil mixed with petrol in tank
	2	Cable ends and levers on handlebars	Any light machine oil
	3	Front brake pin	Any light machine oil
	4	Rear brake attachment	Any light machine oil
Every 1,000 Miles or Monthly	5	Gearbox—check level and top up	Drain and refill after first 500 miles. SAE 20 (Winter) SAE 30 (Summer)
	6	Rear suspension lever and torsion bar (3 points)	Mobilgrease No. 2, Castrolease CL, Shell A, Energrease AO, Retinax, or CD
	7	End of clutch cable	Any light machine oil
	8	Side panel catches (1 each side)	Any light machine oil
	9	End of brake cable	Any light machine oil
	10	Rear brake pedal pivot	Grease as 6
Every 2,000–2,500 Miles (Three-monthly)	11	Rear transmission unit—check level and top up	SAE 140 e.g. Molbilube GX 140, Castrol Hi-Press EP, Shell Spirax 140 EP, Esso Expee 140
	12	Rear brake pivot (can be ignored	Grease as for 6, *but do not overgrease*
	13	Front wheel bearings (each side)	Castrol WB or similar, *do not overgrease*
	14	Front suspension casing	As for 6 (make up grease level)
Every 5,000 Miles (Six-monthly)	15	Handlebar head bearing	⎫ Repack with grease if dismantled and re-assembled
	16	Handlebar bottom bearing	⎭
	17	Cavity for ball-bearing seat	Mobilgrease MP, Castrolease WB, or equivalent. Remove plug near greaser to allow escape of old grease
	5	Gearbox	Drain and refill

either with a grease gun or oilcan. A complete lubrication diagram is given in Fig. 25 with the items numbered and listed in the Lubrication Table.

The gearbox is fitted with three plugs, removable by unscrewing, Fig. 26. The correct oil for the gearbox is SAE 30 for summer, or operation in hot climates overseas, and the slightly thinner grade SAE 20 for winter months, or predominately cold climates. The correct quantity of oil is three-quarters of a pint.

FIG. 26. GEARBOX FILLER-PLUG IS ARROWED. LEVEL PLUG IS AT FRONT AND DRAIN PLUG ON THE UNDERSIDE OF THE CASTING

Gearbox oil should be drained completely and replaced every 5,000 miles. On a brand new machine, make the first change at 500 miles.

With a new machine the original oil should be drained completely from the gearbox after the first 300 to 500 miles by unscrewing first the filler plug and then the drain plug. This oil should be thrown away. Replace the drain plug and add $\frac{3}{4}$ pint of new oil. Thereafter the oil level in the gearbox should be checked every 1,000 miles by removing the filler and level plugs. If there is sufficient oil in the gearbox it will flow readily from the level plug hole. If below this level, add the appropriate grade of oil until it just begins to escape from the level plug hole, replace the level plug and add a further $\frac{1}{4}$ pint of oil, but do not overfill.

When the mileage has reached 5,000, and every 5,000 miles thereafter, drain the gearbox completely and refill with new oil. Alternatively, if your annual mileage is relatively low, arrange to drain the gearbox every six months, say in November, to fill up with new SAE 20 grade oil and in April to refill with SAE 30 oil.

The rear axle unit, Fig. 27, has a maximum oil capacity of $\frac{1}{4}$ pint, the grade of oil required being SAE 140, which is very thick. The level can be checked by removing the filler plug. Check every 2,000 to 2,500 miles and top up, if necessary, until the oil level is visible through the filler plug hole. In cold weather the oil will flow more easily if slightly warmed before attempting to top up. On some 125 c.c. machines there is no filler plug on the rear of the transmission case. The unit is filled through the opening formed by removing the circular side cover, together with the speedometer drive unit, if fitted. Some of the later models have a special breather fitted to the top of the transmission case. It is not a filling point;

decarbonizing. Neither of these may actually be *essential*, but if done at this stage will restore the performance of the machine to near new.

The simpler maintenance jobs can be covered with a minimum of tools. Each new machine is supplied with the following tools as standard equipment—

> Combined spark plug and wheel nut spanner
> Screwdriver
> Rear hub spanner—19 mm. open end
> 8–10 mm. double-ended spanner
> Contact points cleaner (file)
> Tool case.

These tools should normally be carried on the machine in a compartment over the rear wheel.

In addition the following tools and accessories will be found helpful, or necessary, for simple maintenance work: tyre pressure gauge*, oilcan, grease gun, foot pump, small wire brush*, spare sparking plug*.

The items marked with an asterisk are recommended to be carried on the machine.

WEEKLY MAINTENANCE

SPARKING PLUG. Remove the high tension lead and unscrew the spark plug from the cylinder, using the kit spanner, Fig. 28a. The plug points should be cleaned by scrubbing with a small wire brush and the gap checked (Fig. 28b) and re-set, if necessary. The gap should be between 0·015 and 0·020 in. and can be measured with a feeler gauge, or failing this, a stout postcard, Fig. 28c. A double thickness of card torn from a cigarette packet is also about 0·020 in.

It is also good practice to examine the appearance of the spark plug, particularly if the engine has not been running too well. If the points are white and heavily corroded then the type of plug being used is too soft and running could probably be improved by fitting a harder plug. Conversely, if the points and inside of the porcelain insulator seem black and oily, the plug may be too hard. Your local garage can advise on this point, but see also Chapter VII.

TYRE PRESSURES. Pressures in the tyres should be checked weekly and brought up to the correct pressures, if necessary, i.e.—

> front tyre ... 15–16 lb per sq in.
> rear wheel ... 22–24 lb per sq in.
> sidecar version, all wheels ... 25 lb per sq in.

If a spare wheel is carried, re-inflate to 22–24 lb per sq in. if it has fallen below this figure. Pressure values are indicated directly on the stem of the tyre pressure-gauge when the nipple end is pressed firmly over the valve stem of the tyre.

REGULAR MAINTENANCE

its purpose is to prevent excess pressure building up in the casing, an occurence that might force oil past the oil seals on to the rear brake drum and shoes.

Continual, efficient operation of all parts of the machine then, depends upon certain items receiving regular maintenance. No piece of machinery will continue to work indefinitely without attention. If maintenance is neglected entirely, the machine may go on functioning for quite a long period, but eventually a serious defect will develop and need skilled attention to put right, which means a costly repair bill. Regular maintenance not only cuts the cost of such bills and spaces them out at much wider intervals, but it ensures that every part of the machine is kept operating *efficiently* so that the machine is more pleasant, and safer, to drive.

MAINTENANCE

No skilled knowledge of mechanical parts is required to carry out such maintenance jobs. They are all quite straightforward and take very little time to perform. The longer they are neglected the more the machine will suffer. Doing the job for yourself will cost next to nothing and give you increased pride in ownership of your Lambretta.

Whether at a later stage you will want to go on and tackle more advanced maintenance jobs such as dismantling and cleaning the carburettor, adjusting the steering bearings, etc., is entirely a personal choice. These jobs will want doing after some 5,000 miles. You can stop short here and turn such mechanical jobs over to your local service agent. If you prefer to tackle these items as well, then full details are set out in Chapter VI. The main thing is not to neglect any of the items listed.

For convenience, regular maintenance can be split up into separate sections appropriate to different time (or distance) intervals in the life of the machine. Some items, and these are quite minor ones, require a regular weekly check. Others require regular checking at 1,000 mile intervals or, say monthly, whichever is the shorter period of time. After 2,500 miles there are other features that need checking and by 5,000 miles possibly the brake linings may need replacing and the engine

FIG. 27.
REAR BEVEL-GEAR FILLER IS ARROWED. SOME EARLY 125 C.C. MACHINES HAVE NO FILLING POINT HERE

Oil is checked and renewed by removing circular cover on side of transmission case, where the speedometer drive is fitted.

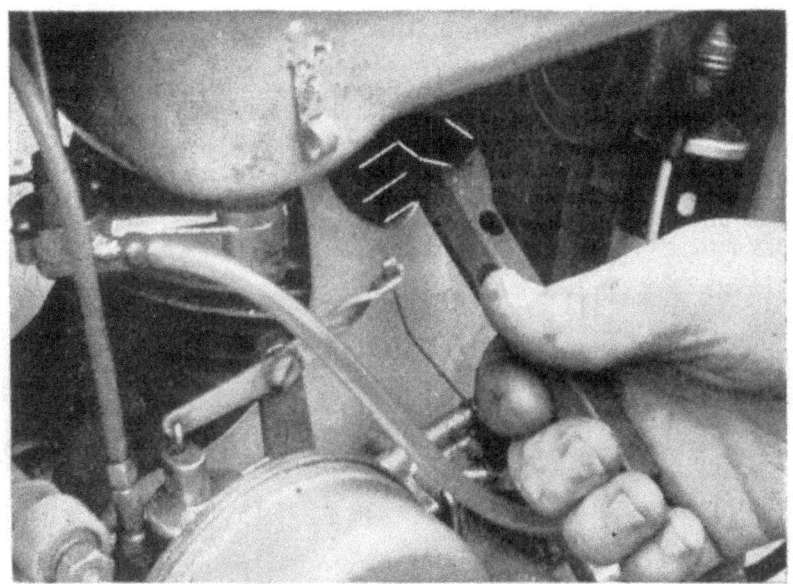

Fig. 28 (a). The Plug is Readily removed with the Cranked Box-spanner Supplied in the Tool Kit
Remove high-tension lead first by pulling off.

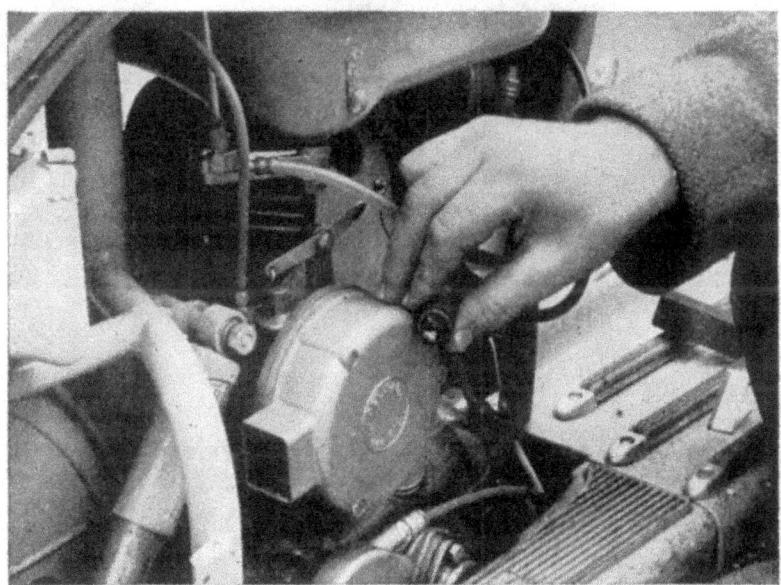

Fig. 28 (b). Check Plug for Spark Before Replacing
But *don't* hold like this. You will get a shock if the engine is turned over. Hold against part of the engine by the insulated lead.

CONTROL CABLES. A drop or two of oil should be applied at each end of the cables where they emerge from their sheathing or outer cover. Pay particular attention to the clutch and front brake levers on the handlebars, but do not over-lubricate.

BRAKES. These should not need adjustment at less than monthly intervals unless the machine is driven a lot and the brakes used excessively (i.e. instead of driving on the throttle). However, check that the brakes are

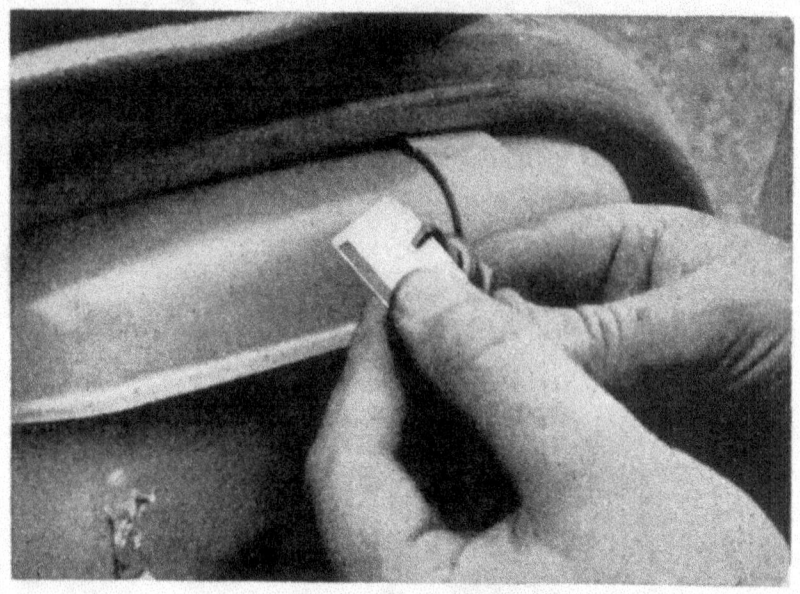

FIG. 28 (c). FAILING FEELER GAUGES, PLUG GAP CAN BE SET CORRECTLY WITH TWO THICKNESSES OF PAPER TORN FROM A CIGARETTE PACKET

Tap bent-over electrode gently to close gap. Keep the points clean. (Use a nail file if you have nothing better.)

operating efficiently and, if not, adjust as described under "1,000 mile maintenance" below.

1,000 MILE OR MONTHLY MAINTENANCE

After 1,000 miles of driving, or every month if the monthly mileage is less than this figure, the following additional items require attention.

GEARBOX. Check the oil level in the gearbox and, if necessary, top up as described above.

CLUTCH. The clutch will probably need adjustment at this stage. This is done by taking up slack in the cable, with the knurled nut provided for

REGULAR MAINTENANCE 47

the purpose, at the handlebar end of the cable, Fig. 29. When all the available adjustment has been taken up by this means, or where no cable adjuster is fitted, it is necessary to adjust from the other end. To do this unscrew the acorn-shaped nut (19 mm size) on the front of the clutch cover. This will expose to view the ball-headed bushing mounted on the clutch pull-rod, locked in place with two 8 mm nuts. Slacken off the first nut, then tighten the second until there is enough take-up when the clutch

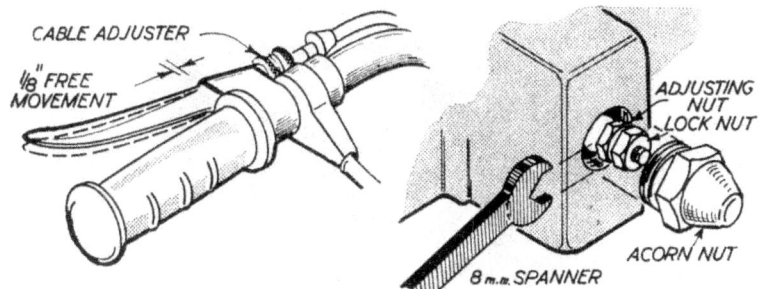

FIG. 29. ADJUSTING THE CLUTCH: BY CABLE ADJUSTERS (LEFT) OR AT CLUTCH ITSELF (RIGHT)

lever is operated. This is judged by the small amount of free movement at the clutch lever end. Lock in this position by tightening down the second nut against the first.

Before replacing the acorn nut start the engine and check that the clutch is both disengaging properly and taking up properly when pulling away in first gear. If not, readjust the two nuts and try again. If no satisfactory adjustment can be found then the clutch will probably need dismantling for further attention (*see* Chapter VI, Section 6).

If the machine has been left idle for some time the clutch may not disengage properly when first trying to get away in gear. This can be due to the clutch plates sticking together with the oil collected on them. In this case the plates may be freed by putting the machine into second gear with the engine stopped, declutching and pushing the machine along for a few yards.

BRAKES. On all models fitted with cable adjusters the front brake can readily be taken up with the adjuster. The rear brake is adjusted by releasing the cable from the end clamp plates and readjusting for length before tightening up the clamp plates again. Where no cable adjuster is fitted to the handlebar end of the front brake, the small clamp locking the lower end of the cable is slackened and cable length readjusted here. On late models with cable adjusters a modified form of cable clamp is fitted at the lower end of the front-brake cable locking the cable end in the form of a loop, Fig. 30. Adjustment of cable length can be made at this point instead of the handlebar adjuster, if preferred. Intermediate models with cable adjusters have the lower end of the front brake cable terminating in a soldered-on nipple and the only adjustment is at the handlebar end.

WHEEL NUTS. These should be checked for tightness at monthly intervals, using the spark plug spanner to tighten up, if necessary. If the nuts appear to be badly rusted, it is recommended that they be unscrewed, cleaned, coated lightly with grease and replaced, one nut at a time. Do not,

FIG. 30. FRONT-BRAKE CABLES ARE ADJUSTABLE AT BOTH ENDS ON LATER MODELS

On early models all the adjustment had to be made at the wheel end. Screwdriver is being used here to spring brake-arm forward to release brake cable, a necessary preliminary to removing the front wheel.

however, remove more than three wheel nuts at a time unless the tyre is first deflated.

THE BATTERY. The acid level in the battery, visible by removing the filler plugs to each cell, Fig. 31, should be checked. If below the top of the separators, top up with distilled water or clean tap water until the separators are just covered. It is most important not to *overfill* the battery, this being a common fault.

If water is spilt on top of the battery when doing this, or when there is any appearance of moisture on the outside of the battery, wipe clean with a dry rag. If the terminals seem at all corroded, remove the leads, clean the terminals and lightly smear the lead connexions and terminals with vaseline before reconnecting.

REGULAR MAINTENANCE

If the battery has been used a lot and is in a partially-discharged condition it will probably pay to remove it and have it fully charged at your local garage. The state of the battery can be judged by switching on the lights and observing how bright they are. If they are relatively dull and tend to fade away, then the battery is in a nearly discharged state.

2,500 MILE, OR THREE MONTHLY MAINTENANCE

GEARBOX. The oil level should be checked and topped up, if necessary.

DECARBONIZING. It is possible, but unlikely at this stage, that a considerable amount of carbon deposit may have collected in the engine,

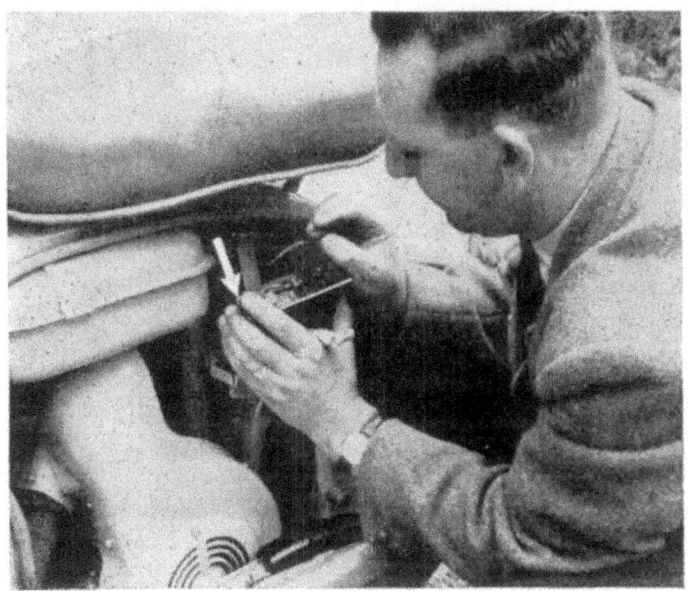

FIG. 31. CHECK THE ACID LEVEL OF THE BATTERY AT REGULAR INTERVALS

If low, top-up with ordinary tap water, but do not overfill. Take special care when handling the battery not to break off the terminal lug (arrowed).

affecting performance. This would be evidenced by a lack of pulling power at the higher speeds. If this trouble is suspected, then decarbonizing the exhaust port may be an effective cure until the 5,000 miles stage. For this the exhaust pipe will have to be detached from the engine. (*See* Chapter VI, Section 4, for details.)

5,000 MILE, OR SIX MONTHLY MAINTENANCE

GEARBOX. The oil should be drained completely and replaced with fresh oil to the correct specification.

REAR AXLE. The oil level should be checked and topped up, if necessary.

DECARBONIZING. Decarbonizing both the engine and silencer will probably be necessary at this stage, although it may often be delayed for a further 2,500 miles. Decarbonizing is not a particularly difficult or skilled job. (*See* Chapter VI, Section 4.) However, many owners may prefer to have this job done by a local service agent.

CARBURETTOR. This should be dismantled, cleaned out thoroughly and replaced. (*See* Chapter VI, Section 12.)

BRAKES. The wheel hubs should be removed and the brake drums and

FIG. 32 (*a*). HAVING RELEASED THE BRAKE CABLE, THE NEXT STEP IN REMOVING THE FRONT WHEEL IS TO SLACKEN THE TWO LARGE NUTS HOLDING THE WHEEL ON THE TRAILING LINKS

linings thoroughly cleaned with petrol. It may also be necessary at this stage to fit replacement shoes and linings, depending on the amount of wear present. (*See* Chapter VI, Section 3.)

CONTACT-BREAKER POINTS. These should be checked and re-adjusted, as necessary. (*See* Chapter VI, Section 10.)

FRONT FORK ASSEMBLY. At this stage there may be a certain amount of looseness in the steering which requires taking up in the steering bearings. (*See* Chapter VI, Section 13.)

It will be appreciated from the above that the 5,000 mile or six-monthly maintenance involves work which the non-technical owner would probably prefer to put out to his local service agent. It should be emphasized, however, that none of the work involved is particularly difficult and can be tackled quite successfully by the average amateur following the specific instructions referenced.

Removing the Wheels. Removing the wheels is a simple process. Once the machine is pulled up on its stand either or both wheels can be removed readily, tipping the machine about its stand, as necessary, for ground clearance.

To remove the front wheel the brake cable must first be disconnected.

FIG. 32 (b). PRISE OUT THE THICK WASHERS FITTING INTO THE DEPRESSION IN THE TRAILING LINKS

If the handlebars are turned full left the wheel can then be removed to the right-hand side. Leaving the nuts on the axle will prevent lost washers.

Cables that terminate in soldered nipples on the cable-end can readily be sprung out by levering on the brake arm with a screwdriver. The two large blind nuts on the ends of the wheel spindle can then be unscrewed (they need not be removed entirely) and the two plain washers behind them pulled out from the recesses in the trailing links. The wheel will then drop out of the trailing links. It is more readily removed from the right-hand side with the handlebars turned fully to the left, Fig. 32a, b and c.

The rim complete with tyre can be detached by unscrewing the three capped nuts. The rim and tyre is then detached from the hub. To remove the tyre the remaining three plain nuts are unscrewed so that the two halves of the rim can be parted, *but before this is done it is essential that the tube be deflated,* otherwise the two halves of the rim will fly apart when the nuts are released. The rim and tyre complete, as originally removed,

FIG. 32 (*c*). THE RIM AND TYRE CAN THEN BE DETACHED BY UNSCREW-
ING THE THREE CAPPED NUTS, BUT DO NOT LOSE THE SPRING WASHERS
BEHIND EACH

The *plain* nuts must not be unscrewed unless the tyre is deflated first.
The front wheel is now interchangeable with the back.

is interchangeable with the rear wheel and thus the spare tyre is common to both.

The rear wheel is removed simply by unscrewing the three cap nuts, after first taking off the left-hand side panel on LC and LD machines, Figs. 33*a* and *b*. Tyre removal is, of course, identical since the rims are identical. Replacing either wheel reverses the procedure, but in replacing the front wheel, particular care must be taken to see that the slot in the

Fig. 33 (a). The Rear Wheel Rim is Removed by Unscrewing the Three Capped Nuts

Fig. 33 (b). The Wheel can then be Lifted Off (knock to free, if stiff) and Manoeuvred Out without Detaching the Left Pillion Foot-rest

It is a good plan to swap front and rear wheels at monthly intervals to equalize tyre wear

brake back plate on the hub registers with the small projection on the inside of the right-hand trailing link. This location serves as an anchor for the brake. If not engaged, application of the brake would simply rotate the back plate and hub and result in damage. On the front-wheel spindle there is also one thin washer to be replaced between the brake back plate and the right trailing link. The two thicker washers are, of course, located in the recess on the outside of each link arm before tightening up the 19 mm spindle nuts.

For further details on dismantling the wheels, *see* Chapter VI, Section 3.

CHAPTER V

TRACING AND CURING FAULTS

WITH EXPERIENCE, and with a working knowledge of the function of the various parts of the Lambretta, the cause or location of such faults as may develop should be fairly obvious. Regular maintenance on the lines detailed in Chapter IV should go a long way to reducing the liability of faults developing. The following tables are designed to locate typical faults against cause and cure, and are intended as a general guide for trouble shooting. Reference should be made to other sections of the book for specific information on the components referred to for adjustment, etc. Most of the simpler faults that may occur can be dealt with by the owner without incurring the service charges involved with professional attention.

Symptom	Cause	Remedy
Engine will not start	(i) Lack of petrol	Check that choke is operated when starting engine from cold. Check that petrol tap is turned on. Check that there is petrol in the tank.
	(ii) Too much petrol (engine flooded)	A strong smell of petrol will be present near the carburettor and the outside of the carburettor may be quite wet. The trouble is that the mixture drawn in has not been fired by the plug. Check as for (iii).
	(iii) Lack of spark	Take out plug and see if wet (condition (ii) above), or excessively dirty. Clean plug and readjust points, if necessary. If engine already flooded, kick over smartly half a dozen times before replacing plug. If plug is still not sparking, remove again and hold against side of engine and kick engine over. Check that a good "hot" spark jumps the plug gap. If not, remove lead and check that spark will jump $\frac{1}{16}$ in. to $\frac{1}{4}$ in. to engine casing. If lead sparks but plug does not, fit a new plug. If lead does not give proper spark, check under ignition fault (iv).
	(iv) Ignition trouble (other than plug)	Remove flywheel domed cover and check points for: (a) incorrect gap, (b) points dirty or worn. Adjust or correct, as necessary. Check for broken, bared or disconnected leads to coil (green wires) or earth lead (black) broken off from crankcase.

56 THE BOOK OF THE LAMBRETTA MOTOR-SCOOTER

Symptom	Cause	Remedy
Engine starts but stops soon after	(i) Lack of petrol	If the petrol tap is not turned on the engine may start on the petrol in the carburettor but will run out of fuel very soon after. Check that there is petrol in the tank.
	(ii) Ignition fault	Check wires for loose connexions.
	(iii) Engine too cold	This is likely to occur only in very cold weather if the choke is closed immediately the engine starts to run. Start again with throttle quarter open.
Engine runs badly (idling and moderate speeds)	(i) Incorrect mixture	Adjust idling screws on carburettor. Check for dirt in carburettor or in fuel line. Check that throttle slide in carburettor is not sticking. Check and clean carburettor jets.
	(a) Mixture too lean	Check for air leaks, e.g. carburettor top loose, gaskets faulty, etc. Check that vent hole in petrol-tank filler cap is not blocked.
	(b) Mixture too rich	Check that choke has not been left out. Check that atomizer jet is not enlarged. Check that carburettor float has not stuck or become "holed" and sunk.
	(ii) Ignition fault	Check plug first, then contact breaker. Observe plug to see if type is matched to engine (see Chapter VII).
Engine runs badly (engine speeds)	(i) Poor carburation	Check as above. Check also that carburettor is vertical, not displaced, causing float to stick.
	(ii) Ignition fault	Check as above. Check that contact breaker arm is not seized or stiff on its pin. Check that contact-breaker spring is intact and not too weak. Condenser may be faulty (unlikely). Stator may be faulty (earthed).
Engine lacks pulling power	(i) Poor carburation	Check as above.
	(ii) Ignition fault	Check as above.
	(iii) Engine blocked with carbon	Engine and silencer needs decarbonizing (not before 3,000 miles on a new machine or 5–6,000 miles if the machine is driven hard.
	(iv) Mixture too rich	A common fault with learners is to leave the choke out accidentally.
	(v) Silencer	Baffle plates reassembled wrong way.
Engine stops when lights switched on	Faulty ignition adjustments	Either the plug gap is too large or contact-breaker gap too large or too small. Readjust to cure.
Engine noise		Try to trace the region from which the noise is coming. A different noise from normal engine noise is usually an indication of something faulty which should be attended to at once, otherwise there is the chance of serious internal damage resulting.
	(i) Screaming noise from any part	Usually a sign of complete lack of lubrication. At first it will appear intermittently, but if ignored may result in complete failure of the part affected.

TRACING AND CURING FAULTS   57

Symptom	Cause	Remedy
Noise (general)	(ii) Rattling noise from magneto	Check if the cover plate is loose. On a Marelli type magneto with automatic advance and retard the spring may be weak. The rattle will be noticeable at idling speeds only.
	(iii) Rattle from silencer	Silencer may have worked loose. Re-tighten.
	(iv) Excess noise from silencer	Silencer casing split. Must be replaced (or welded repair done).
	Whining noise from— (a) Engine gears	Too much clearance on engine bevel and clutch bevel. Requires remeshing with shims (see Chapter VI, Section 8).
	(b) Gearbox	Too much clearance on gears or worn or damaged gears. Check as per Chapter VI, Section 8.
	(c) Kick-starter gears	Clearance incorrect. Readjust with new thickness of gasket.
	(d) Crown wheel and pinion	Clearance incorrect. Should be 0·002 to 0·004 in. Readjust with paper gasket between backplate and transmission case.
Gears	Stiff to operate	Cable requires lubricating.
	Slips out of top gear	Check for kinks in cable; readjust eccentric in gearbox.
	Slips out of 1st gear	Adjust eccentric in gearbox.
Throttle stiff	Twist grip is binding	Tap in slightly towards the centre of the handlebars the bracket holding the front brake, to free it.
Throttle does not close	Twist grip free, but does not shut off automatically	Spring broken in carburettor.
Self-starter does not work	Battery run down	Check condition of battery.
	Starter leads faulty	Check switch on top of starter for oil impregnation, and leads to switch for corrosion
Self-starter runs but engine does not start	(i) Fuse blown	The fuse will not normally blow unless there is a fault developed on the electrical circuit. Look for this before replacing fuse. It is possible that a fuse with too low a rating was fitted (8 amp maximum).
	(ii) Ignition or carburation fault	Check as for standard model if fuse is intact.
No lights	Disconnected lead(s)	Look for loose connexions or wires broken off.
Clutch	Slips when in gear	Readjust, at handlebar end first (where screw adjusters fitted); then by the two 8 mm nuts at the clutch end (see Chapter VI, Section 8). If not cured, springs may be weak or clutch linings worn below useful limit.
	Does not engage	Most probably due to seized cable.
	Sticks	May be due to oil on plates acting as an adhesive after machine has stood idle for some time. Effect will disappear almost at once. If not, readjust.
Brakes	Poor stopping power	Readjust to take up wear. When no further readjustment remains, replace shoes and bonded linings.

THE BOOK OF THE LAMBRETTA MOTOR-SCOOTER

Symptom	Cause	Remedy
Brakes (contd.)		Oil on linings and drum. Oil seals may be faulty on rear hub. Clean linings and drums with petrol and scour linings with emery or sandpaper.
	One brake more effective than the other	The front brake will seem to be more effective for stopping on dry surfaces since a greater proportion of the weight of the machine is transferred to the front wheel in braking. A poor performance of one brake relative to the other almost certainly means that this brake is used most and requires more frequent readjustment, or has worn to the point where new linings are required.
No parking lights	Fuse blown	Check for possible shorts causing fuse to blow.
Parking lights weak	Battery low	Recharge battery. Check charging rate.
	Faulty rectifier	Check back current (not more than 3 milliamps).
No charge	Fuse blown	Check and replace (as above).
Weak charge	Faulty rectifier	Replace if faulty.
	Magneto demagnetized	Remagnetizing service available.
	Lighting coil faulty	Check for disconnected leads. Stator may be earthed.
Poor lights (running)	Excessive bulb wattage	Check against bulb schedule (see Chapter VII).
Poor headlamp beam	Magneto demagnetized	
	Reflector damaged (see also "Poor Lights" above)	Reflector damaged by fingering or burnt by using headlamp bulb of excessive wattage (above 24 watts).
No lights (running)	Disconnexion	Check for disconnected lead or faulty lighting coil. Stator may be earthed or partially earthed.
Horn does nor work	Disconnexion	Check for disconnected lead. NOTE. Since the electrical systems differ on the various models, refer to the wiring diagrams in Chapter VII for further details.
Steering erratic	Wrong tyre pressures	Check pressures and readjust as necessary.
	Forks deformed	Straighten or replace forks.
	Wheel loose	Unlikely but check.
	Steering bearings loose	Remove handlebars and tighten.

CHAPTER VI

DETAILED MAINTENANCE AND ADJUSTMENT

THE LAMBRETTA MODELS employ metric sizes of threads, nuts and bolts throughout. A complete range of tools is marketed by Lambretta Concessionaires, although metric-size spanners are readily available from most good tool stockists. In this respect it should be remembered that *size* as specified for metric nuts and bolts refers to the width of the hexagon across the flats and not, as is standard British practice, the diameter of the bolt.

1. TOOL KITS

A complete servicing tool kit for Lambretta models can be subdivided into two main groups. The first comprises a set of standard tools and extractors which will cover all normal maintenance requirements, the complete set costing about £10. The second comprises a set of special tools necessary for complete dismantling at an additional cost of some £20. Although all these special tools are not essential in that, for example, some other form of punch or holder can be improvised for a particular job, certain dismantling jobs are either tedious, or even impossible, without them. With a complete set of special tools, in fact, complete dismantling of the Lambretta engine is comparatively simple and straightforward, despite its apparent complexity.

Complete servicing tool kits are, of course, maintained by Lambretta servicing agents. The purchase of such tools by individual clubs for loan to members makes it possible for an individual owner to tackle complete stripping of his engine, transmission and suspension without involving himself in the appreciable capital outlay otherwise necessary (*see* Chapter IX). The tools required for normal maintenance work are shown in Fig. 34*a* and the additional tools needed for complete dismantling are illustrated in Fig. 34*b*.

2. CABLES

On all models it is normally possible to disconnect, remove and replace all control cables without dismantling any other parts of the machine. On LDA models and very late LD models the inner brake cables may be withdrawn from the outer sheathing by disconnecting at the screw connexion at the end remote from the handlebars. On all LD models the throttle cable passes down inside the front cowl and, if stuck, it is sometimes necessary to remove the cowl to replace the cable. This is done by removing the one screw at the bottom of the headlamp rim and removing

60 THE BOOK OF THE LAMBRETTA MOTOR-SCOOTER

the rim to gain access to the two screws behind the reflector holding the top of the cowl to the leg shield. The lower part of the cowl is held by two screws fitted behind the leg shield.

Brakes. The rear brake is controlled by a thick cable on all but the earlier machines. Both adjustment and replacement of this cable are

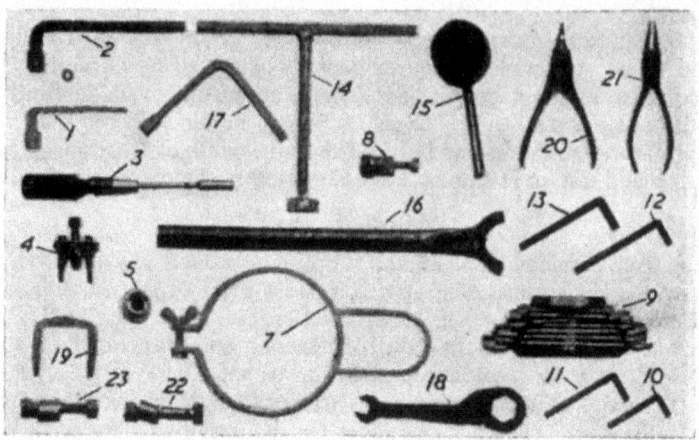

FIG. 34 (a). A COMPLETE SET OF LAMBRETTA TOOLS FOR NORMAL MAINTENANCE WORK

1. Cylinder-head spanner (125 c.c.).
2. Cylinder-head spanner (150 c.c.).
3. 8 mm handled socket spanner (for footboards, carburettor and general use).
4. Rear-hub extractor.
5. 19 mm socket for flywheel.
6. 19 mm socket (as above) with bar.
7. Flywheel holder.
8. Flywheel extractor.
9. Set of open-ended metric spanners (sizes 7, 8, 9, 10, 12, 14, 17, 19, 21, 24 and 27 mm).
10. Small Allen key 3·5 mm (for detachable cable nipples).
11. Small Allen key 4·5 mm (for headlamp and horn).
12. Small Allen key 5 mm (for clutch, transmission and kick-starter cases).
13. Small Allen key 6 mm (for transmission case).
14. Tank-neck spanner (125 c.c.).
15. Tank-neck spanner (150 c.c.).
16. Silencer-neck spanner.
17. Oil-plug tool.
18. 27 mm spanner (for rear-wheel nut).
19. Clutch compressor.
20. Circlip pliers (contracting).
21. Circlip pliers (expanding).
22. Small-end bush extractor (14 mm).
23. Small-end bush extractor (16 mm).

straightforward and obvious; it is freed from the rear end first. On the earlier rod-operated system the adjuster was locked by a right-hand nut at one side and a left-hand nut at the other, Fig. 35.

The handlebar assembly differs in detail on 1954 and later LD models, also between the 125 c.c. and 150 c.c. machines. Machines of this type may or may not have cable adjusters on the handlebar ends for the clutch and front brake cables (*See* Fig. 29). On models fitted with adjusters, the brake cable should be slackened right off at the adjuster when the bottom end, which terminates in a soldered-on nipple, can be sprung out of the brake arm with a screwdriver or similar tool. Later versions with cable adjusters have the cable end made off in a loop secured in a clamp which may be slackened and the cable freed accordingly. Systems without

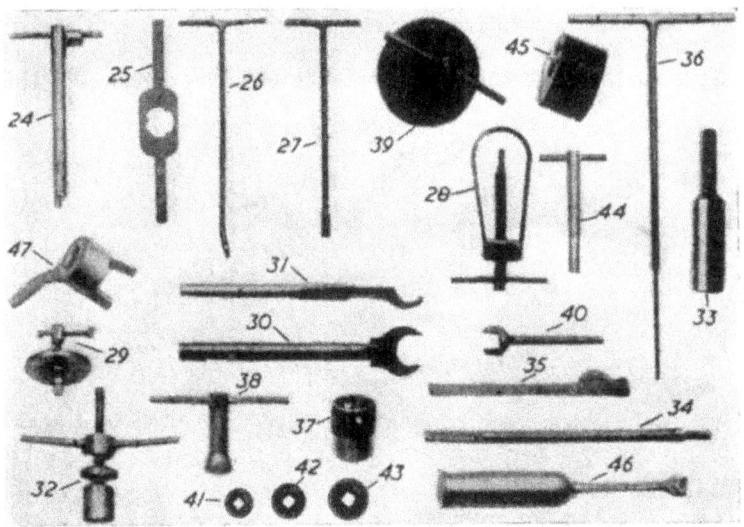

FIG. 34 (*b*). EXTRA LAMBRETTA TOOLS FOR COMPLETE DISMANTLING

24. Torsion bar loading tool.
25. Clutch splined collar holder.
26. Jointed 5 mm Allen key.
27. Big-end spanner (125 c.c.).
28. Gudgeon-pin extractor (125 c.c.).
29. Clutch-bell puller.
30. Steering-head spanner.
31. Steering-head spanner.
32. Rear-pinion extractor.
33. Rear-pinion assembly punch.
34. Rear-drive dismantling punch.
35. Clutch-bearing extractor lever.
36. Long 6 mm Allen key.
37. Gear mesher.
38. 27 mm crankshaft-socket spanner (150 c.c.).
39. Magneto-flange extractor.
40. Clutch-sleeve holder.
41. 14 mm socket spanner (for general use).
42. 17 mm socket spanner (for nut on drive side of crankshaft).
43. 24 mm socket spanner (for nut on clutch bell).
44. Crankshaft aligning mandrel (125 c.c.).
45. Spark-timing device.
46. Grease gun.
47. Crankshaft holding-tool.

adjusters have the bottom end of the cable held by a small clamp which must be slackened to release the end of the cable.

Once the lower end of the cable is freed the handlebar lever can be removed by taking off the hinge pin and nut; the cable end can then be slid out of the lever. The lever should not be freed without first detaching the lower end of the cable, otherwise the plastic sheathing is likely to be damaged in trying to work enough slack into the cable to disconnect it from the lever. The split cable stop is readily removed from either end, once there is slack in the cable, by pulling the inner cable away from the outer casing and slipping off the stop. Once the cable is freed from the lever it is then possible to feed the upper cable end (without unscrewing the adjuster, when fitted) through the handlebar bracket.

The cable is best fed back by hand through the rubber grommet in the front mudguard and the two small lugs on the front forks. It should then be possible to withdraw the cable and outer casing complete from the plastic sheath. If not, the headlamp rim and lamp holder should be detached so that the cable can be worked through this opening. When the

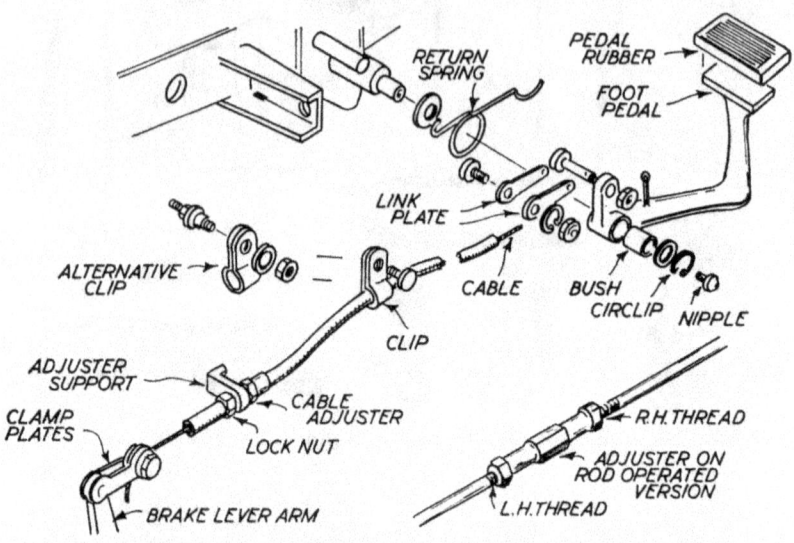

Fig. 35. The Various Parts Forming the Rear Brake Linkage are Shown Here

Rod operation was used on C and LC models and some of the earlier 125 c.c. D and LD machines.

cable is replaced, it is imperative that the outer casing be well greased to allow it to slip through the plastic sheathing.

Clutch. The clutch cable can be dismantled in a similar manner, first releasing it at the engine end. The clutch arm is pulled forwards using a spanner or screwdriver as a lever and the cable nipple slipped off. The clutch lever mechanism at the handlebar end is essentially similar to that of the front brake but is mounted on the twist-grip (gear change) control and thus rotates with it.

Twist-grip Controls. The two twist-grip controls are similar to each other but are appreciably different on 150 c.c. models from those on the

DETAILED MAINTENANCE AND ADJUSTMENT 63

125 c.c. models and earlier 150 c.c. models. In all cases the throttle cable can be removed from either end, but the gear-change cable should be removed from the selector-box end. To do this the selector-box holding-screws must be removed, the circlip detached from the end of the selector spindle which, together with the selector box and selector arm, are removed as a unit. The cable adjusters can then be removed and the cable released from the selector arm. On models fitted with screw type connectors the cable can be released from the nipple by unscrewing the nipple grub-screw.

The type of twist-grip typical of the 125 c.c. machines is shown in Fig. 36. The handlebar is slotted along the length of the grip and an inner

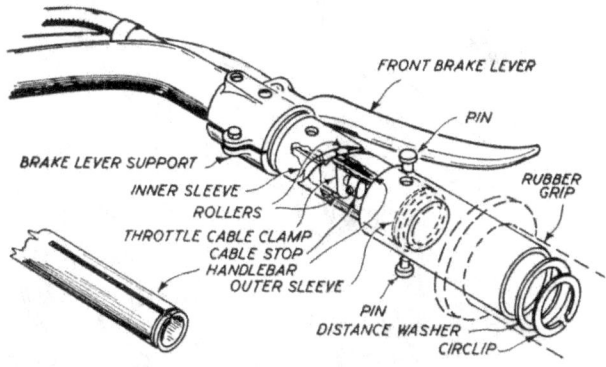

FIG. 36. TWIST-GRIP CONTROL (THROTTLE) ON THE 125 C.C. LAMBRETTA

A helical cut-out in the inner sleeve provides push-pull motion for the cable. Gear-shift control is similar, with thicker Teleflex cable to operate effectively both "pushing" and "pulling".

sleeve cut with a helical slot at 45 degrees fits over it. The cable is anchored in the handlebar slot and inner sleeve helix a fitting which has two small rollers, rotation of the inner sleeve causing the cable to be pulled along inside the handlebar. The return action is by means of the spring in the carburettor, the inner sleeve rotating back in an anticlockwise direction. The inner sleeve is locked on to the handlebars with a circlip with spacing washers at each end. An outer sleeve fits over the inner sleeve and is secured with two small grub pins or pegs, these being held in place by the rubber grip which fits over the whole assembly. The gear-change, twist-grip control is essentially similar on the left-hand handle bar except that a much thicker Teleflex control cable is employed. This is rigid enough to work effectively with both a "push" and a "pull" action. In both cases the cables emerge from the handlebars immediately inside the first bend where they enter the moulded plastic sheathing.

Either twist grip can be dismantled by pulling off the rubber grip, removing the grub pins and sliding off the outer sleeve. The brake-lever clamp, or gear-indicator clamp in the gear-change unit, can then be slackened and this unit slid inwards, together with the inner part of the twist grip. The small circlip which prevents movement of the twist-grip sleeve can then be removed. The cable nipple fits into a brass slider through which passes a pin. This pin has a pair of small rollers mounted on it at each end, always assembled with the larger of the rollers next to the slider. The throttle grip is spring loaded towards the close position and so the front brake clamp should be repositioned with enough slack to allow this spring operation to be effective. Alternatively, if a "stiff" throttle is

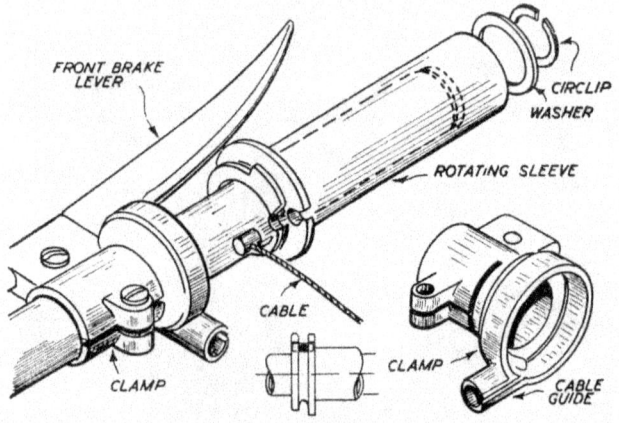

FIG. 37. THROTTLE TWIST-GRIP CONTROL OF 150 c.c. MACHINES

A rubber grip fits over the rotating sleeve. Cable emerges at right angles to handlebars, not through them as on the 125 c.c. models.

preferred, the front-brake clamp can be slackened off, tapped hard up against the handgrip distance washer and retightened in this position.

On the 150 c.c. models both twist-grip controls operate on a direct rotary movement, Figs. 37 and 38, utilizing two cables in the gear change control and one on the throttle side, with spring return action by the carburettor spring, as before. These two control cables therefore feed back at right angles from the handlebars to enter their respective plastic sheathings.

For the single-throttle cable, slackening of the front-brake clamp and sliding it along towards the centre of the handlebars enables the cable end to be unlocked from the throttle sleeve. It actually fits into a grooved flange, the groove taking the lay of the cable under rotary movement of the throttle sleeve.

On the gear-change sleeve shoulder the two cables are when roughly diametrically opposed, locked in place so that whichever way the grip is rotated one cable is in tension and thus provides the necessary "pull" movement at the selector end. The gear-change cables must be released at the selector end before the cables can conveniently be sprung out of the handlebar fitting (*see* above).

A feature commonly overlooked is that if the clamp bracket is not re-tightened close against the rotating sleeve, particularly on the throttle side, the throttle sleeve will have a sideways freedom of movement. In the 125 c.c. system this may completely nullify the action of the twist-grip if the sideways movement is appreciable. What then happens is, that as the sleeve is rotated, instead of the helix in the inner sleeve drawing the cable end along, it remains stationary and the whole sleeve slides inwards

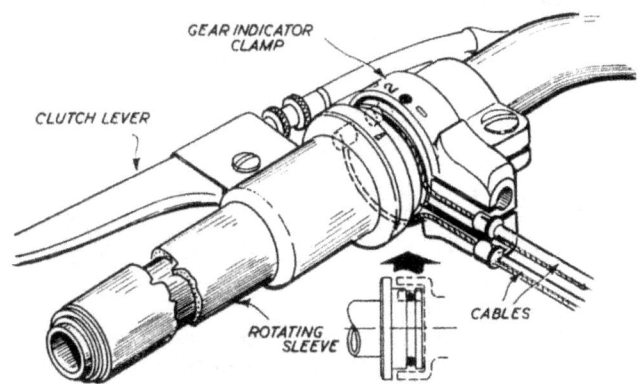

Fig. 38. Gear-shift Control on 150 c.c. Machines is Similar, Except that Two Cables are Used

Again these emerge at right angles to handlebars and enter plastic sheathing. Clutch lever is mounted on rotating sleeve.

against the clamp. This cannot happen in the 150 c.c. throttle, and quite a large gap can be tolerated without experiencing any trouble, although if the gap is too large there is always the possibility of the cable end pulling out of the sleeve-end flange. It is a point worth while checking, particularly if the machine has fallen over and received a knock on the ends of the handlebars, although, actually, a knock on the end of the brake or clutch lever would be necessary to displace the clamp. There should be no appre-ciable sideways movement on either twist-grip, only freedom for rotary movement.

It is usually only necessary to replace the flexible inner cable on all controls; the outer casing and plastic sheathing can be left undisturbed. If desired, however, these items may be removed, taking care not to damage the plastic sheathing, and well greasing the outer casing before replacing. A new inner gear cable, when fitted, should be attached to the selector box end first, splaying it out and soldering it to the nipple, if no nipple is attached; or locking it with the nipple grub-screw where there is a screw-connector nipple. The selector box is then refitted and adjustment taken right off. The free end of the cable at the handlebar end is then drawn tight and the nipple threaded on and soldered in the correct position. Excess length of cable is cut off and splayed back over the nipple, and resoldered for maximum strength. A similar procedure is followed in replacing the throttle cable.

3. BRAKES

Adjustment of the front and rear brakes has already been described in the chapter dealing with regular maintenance. Earlier models had the small cable clamp fitted to the lower end of the front-brake cable with a 11 mm nut. This was followed by eliminating adjustment at this point, terminating the cable in a nipple, and fitting adjusters to the handlebar end of the cable. The latest change is to retain the handlebar adjusters but to re-introduce at the wheel end of the cable a clamp through which the cable is looped and locked, thus allowing adjustment to be made at the lower end, if required.

With the earlier 125 c.c. models the front brake diameter was different from the rear brake but all later models have interchangeable brake shoes and linings. Rear brake shoes and linings are interchangeable on all models. Hub and backplates are also identical on all models produced subsequent to October, 1954.

Removal of the wheels has already been described in Chapter IV. Removal of the brakes, e.g. to clean or change the shoes and linings, is different for the front and rear wheels.

To remove the front-wheel brakes the complete wheel is first detached, the outer blind nuts and thick washers being taken right off. The spindle nuts can then be unscrewed simultaneously with a spanner at each end, and the backplate withdrawn. This exposes the brake shoes which are removed by detaching the circlip on the end of the brake pivot and then withdrawing the shoes before removing the spring. In reassembling, connect the shoes with the spring first and then slide on to the pivot pin, replacing the retaining circlip. If the backplate is a tight fit and does not come off easily it can be released by tapping the wheel spindle with a wooden mallet, or block of hardwood, towards the nearside. Do *not* tap the end of the spindle with a hammer, otherwise you will almost certainly burr over the threads.

In reassembling the hub unit it is important that the two nuts at the ends of the spindle should be screwed up really tight against each other otherwise the assembly may work loose. If it is found on refitting the wheel that the backplate is scraping against the revolving drum, then a thin washer may be fitted on the spindle inside the backplate to increase the clearance. This is often a necessary feature on new machines.

Access to the rear brake shoes and linings is obtained by removing

DETAILED MAINTENANCE AND ADJUSTMENT 69

to which is normally attached an extension pipe with expansion chamber. This type of silencer was also made with a perforated sleeve surrounding the entry chamber packed with glass wool. This, however, has been abandoned since it had a tendency to rattle and did not materially improve the performance of the silencer.

The parts of the silencer are held together with a rod passing right through the centre and the end caps are detachable once the retaining nuts are removed. The baffle and tube assembly can then be withdrawn for cleaning by pulling on the tube from the exhaust-pipe side.

The interior of the silencer can be cleaned by scraping. The far side

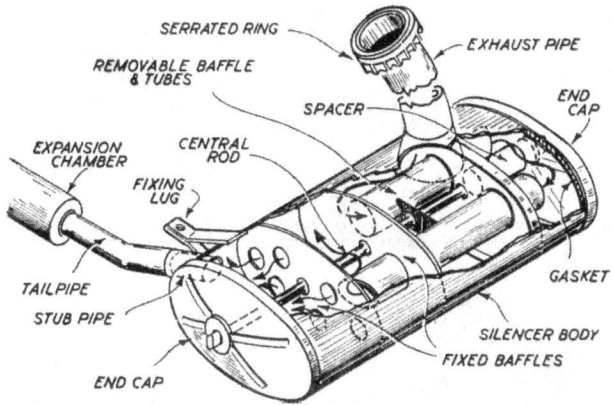

FIG. 39. THE STANDARD-TYPE LAMBRETTA SILENCER WHICH WILL FIT ALL MODELS

An earlier version of this pattern had a perforated inner lining and glass-wool packing, since abandoned. End caps can be removed to withdraw baffle and tubes for decoking.

cover gives access to the tailpipe area which is frequently the most heavily-deposited region. The inside of the stub tailpipe can, of course, also be reached for cleaning merely by removing the tailpipe extension without dismantling the silencer itself.

In reassembling the silencer it is important that the baffle and tubes are assembled the right way round, thus providing free passage for the expansion and exit of the exhaust gases. The end caps are also tightly sealed to the body of the silencer with asbestos string packing which should be renewed, if necessary. The silencer can then be refitted to the engine. This must be done before attempting to replace the engine cowling.

A further type of silencer has been introduced on the latest models (again interchangeable on all engines) in which the body unit is a welded assembly joined around a flanged equator. This silencer gives a better engine performance. Only a short tailpipe of relatively small diameter is fitted to this silencer. It can be removed for cleaning by unscrewing the nut at the extreme end and pulling off the pipe. Two large plugs with hexagonal keys are fitted at the nearside end of the silencer body for access to the interior for cleaning (*see* Fig. 40).

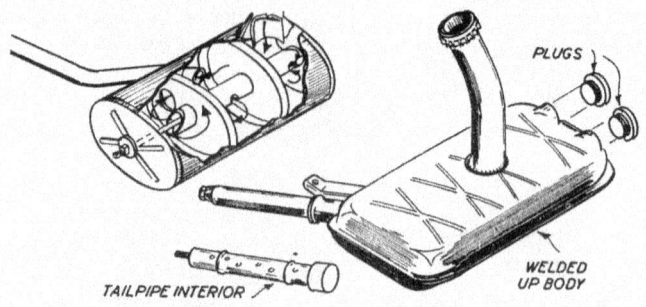

FIG. 40. LEFT-HAND SKETCH SHOWS AN EARLIER FORM OF SILENCER USED ON 125 C.C. MACHINES

Latest pattern (to fit any model) cannot be taken apart, except for short tailpipe. No expansion chamber is used with this type.

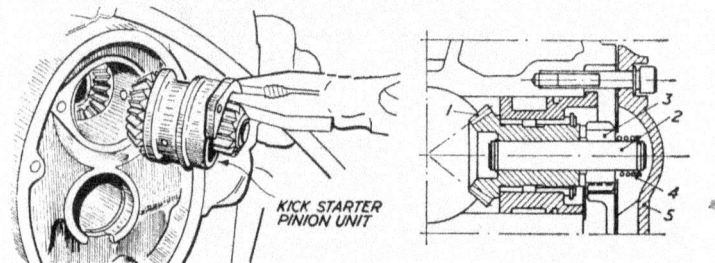

FIG. 41. LEFT-HAND SKETCH SHOWS 125 C.C. PATTERN KICK-STARTER UNIT

A modified version with the spring on the outside and extended spindle (right-hand diagram) was used on early 150 c.c. machines. Small swelling in cover plate accommodated spindle extension.

Key
1. Bevel pinion. 4. Spring.
2. Spindle. 5. Cover plate.
3. Kick-starter pinion.

5. KICK-STARTER UNIT

The kick-starter unit, Figs. 41 and 42, has been subject to a number of modifications but the general arrangement is much the same in all of them. The plain bush mounting of the starter pinion with the spring on the inside of the assembly is standard on all 125 c.c. machines. The spindle, however, was extended and the spring mounted on the outside on the early 150 from the spindle the complete back wheel and hub, without slackening any of the rim nuts. To do this the central nut on the rear hub is unscrewed after first removing the locking screw, which has a left-hand thread, where fitted. This locking screw is standard on later models but earlier models have a slotted wheel nut, to remove which requires a special spanner, supplied with the tool kit.

Once this large nut has been removed the wheel can be knocked off, no special extractor tool being required. A sharp tap on the end of the spindle with a wooden mallet will usually free the hub. Alternatively a block of wood can be laid against the *rim* on the opposite side of the wheel and tapped smartly. It is important, if this method is employed, to place the wooden block against the rim and not the brake-drum fins which are cast aluminium and will break if maltreated. The hub itself is a taper fit on the axle and once started is readily withdrawn. The locking key is normally a tight fit in the axle and so will not drop out. It should, however, be removed and put in a safe place so that it can be found and replaced when re-fitting the wheel. The brake shoes thus exposed can be dismantled and reassembled like the front shoes. In replacing the wheel, fit the key into the axle keyway first and position the wheel on this. Check that the hub is correctly locked on to the axle before replacing the main nut.

4. DECARBONIZING

Decarbonizing demands partial dismantling of the engine and removal of the spark plug, tank, nearside pillion footrest, carburettor, engine cowling and silencer, in that order.

The tank is held by a large ring nut, which requires a special tool to undo, around the filler stem and either one 14 mm acorn nut under the saddle, or one 8 mm bolt at the rear and one 10 mm nut at the front, depending on the model. Detach the plastic fuel line and then remove the tap knob by detaching the spring clip holding it to the tap spindle. It should then be possible to remove the tank by rotating it from under the wing out on the nearside.

The pillion foot-rest is held by four 8 mm nuts. The carburettor fits over the intake manifold extension on the engine cylinder and is locked by a clamp bolt. If this bolt (8 mm) is loosened the carburettor may be pulled off, and the throttle cable may also be detached, for convenience, so that the carburettor may be laid aside in a safe place.

The engine cowling halves are held together with three screws, and a bottom pinch bolt fastens the bottom aluminium flange to the magneto flange, located by the terminal block. This pinch bolt is difficult to get at, but needs only to be slackened off with a screwdriver. The top one of the other three screws is also difficult to reach. The cowling, however, may be removed as a whole by detaching the two accessible screws, pulling the cowling and sliding it clear to the nearside, the two halves still joined by the remaining screw.

The silencer is connected to the exhaust manifold with a serrated ring nut which is unscrewed either with a "C" spanner, or a hammer and a suitable drift. It is preferable to use a block of hard wood than a metal tool. There is also a bracket on the silencer body secured to a lug on the crankcase with a 10 mm nut, which must be detached. The silencer extension must also be free from its anchor lug before the whole unit can be detached.

The cylinder head can be removed by unscrewing the four nuts (10 mm on the 125 c.c. engine; 11 mm on the 150 c.c. engine) with a socket spanner and lifting the head off the four long studs. There is a head gasket (compression plate) on the 125 c.c. engines but this can be discarded after the full running-in period, 1,000 miles, to effect a slight increase in performance. 150 c.c. engines have a small aluminium gasket which *must* be refitted.

The cylinder barrel can now be lifted and withdrawn, exposing all the necessary components for de-carbonizing. It may be more convenient to remove the piston, first removing the circlips from each side of the gudgeon pin and then driving out the gudgeon pin with a suitable drift. The piston fit is usually, and correctly, fairly free. A paper gasket is fitted at the base of the cylinder and should be saved, or renewed if damaged.

All 150 c.c. C models, D models prior to engine number 22865, and LD models prior to engine number 127815, have a 14 mm gudgeon pin. Later models have a 16 mm gudgeon pin as standard. (*See also* Section 11 on "Crankshaft," where replacement parts are called for, since crankshaft replacements are available only with 16 mm small-end bearings.)

Carbon deposits should be scraped clean from the inside of the cylinder head and exhaust outlet; also from the crown of the piston. The piston is of softer metal and more readily scratched, unless care is taken. The piston rings should be removed and the grooves thoroughly cleaned out. Damaged or worn rings should be replaced, checking that when the rings are reassembled they are correctly located with respect to the pegs in the piston grooves. This is an item to check immediately before sliding the cylinder barrel back over the piston, after refitting to the connecting rod, if that was removed initially. The cylinder and head can then be reassembled, reversing the dismantling procedure. The head nuts should be tightened down diagonally and progressively after first running on all nuts finger tight. Make sure that the barrel is reassembled with the sparking plug on the correct side.

The Silencer. The silencer has been developed through a series of different versions. An early model typical of those used on 125 c.c. machines is shown in Fig. 40 and the current standard in Fig. 39. The latter is adaptable to any type of engine and is fitted with a stub tailpipe

DETAILED MAINTENANCE AND ADJUSTMENT 71

c.c. models, Fig. 41, an external difference being a dome-shaped swelling on the kick-starter housing to accommodate the greater spindle length.

A further variation on 150 c.c. machines was then to mount the starter spindle on ball races, but this was confined to only a few machines. The final variation, shown in Fig. 42, was to transfer the ball mounting to a single race held in a separate, detachable housing of triangular shape,

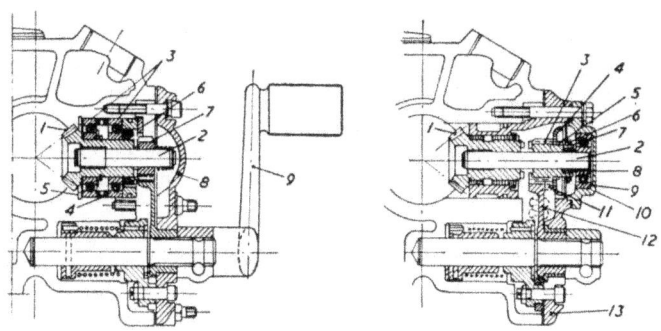

FIG. 42. AN INTERIM DEVELOPMENT WAS THE BALL-RACE MOUNTING (LEFT)

Few, if any, machines of this type reached this country.

Key

1. Bevel pinion.
2. Spindle.
3. Ball-races.
4. Spacer.
5. Seeger ring.

6. Outer plate.
7. Kick-starter pinion.
8. Cover plate.
9. Kick-starter pedal arm.

THE LATER TYPE UNIT ADOPTED FOR THE 150 C.C. MODELS IS SHOWN ON THE RIGHT

Here the single ball-race is mounted in a separate detachable cover.

Key

1. Bevel pinion.
2. Spindle.
3. Kick-starter pinion.
4. Cup.
5. Spring.
6. Thrust washer.
7. Circlip.

8. Spring.
9. Ball-race.
10. Detachable cover.
11. Shoulder in kick-starter quadrant.
12. Kick-starter quadrant.
13. Kick-starter group cover plate.

secured to the main cover plate. In this version the end of the quadrant is fitted with a small projection which engages with a spring-loaded shoulder on the starter pinion. The effect of this is that when the quadrant has advanced to engage the first tooth the ratchet is disengaged. A still later variation is in the design of the ratchet itself, which utilizes a certain amount of free movement between the teeth, produced by the form of the teeth used. A spring on the quadrant then takes up this free movement, as necessary, to ensure correct meshing of the two gears when the quadrant is rotated, i.e. eliminating the possibility of point to point contact of the teeth.

The kick-starter cover plate is held by five screws, three of which or more, depending on the type, may be removed with a 10 mm spanner. The screw at the apex of the group of three at the bottom should not be removed, since this is merely a fixing point for the kick-starter return spring and is, in fact, splayed over inside behind a nut.

The cover plate, together with the kick-starter arm, can be withdrawn, by tapping the inside of the starter arm if necessary. In 125 c.c. models and early 150's, the bevel pinion can be withdrawn by loosening the two 8 mm screws holding the support on to the crankcase unit. On later 150 c.c. models the bevel pinion comes away as one unit after removing the casing.

The toothed quadrant which engages with this pinion is fitted on to a splined length of the starter shaft. Quadrant and shaft are loaded to return to normal position by $1\frac{1}{2}$ turns rotation of a coil spring, one end of which is secured to an aluminium tensioning plate on the apex screw mentioned above. This tensioning plate is drilled with a hole through which a tommy bar can be inserted to preload the spring $1\frac{1}{2}$ turns should the quadrant be dismantled and reassembled. In this case the tensioning plate would be turned $1\frac{1}{2}$ times anticlockwise and held in this position while the quadrant is tapped back on to the splined end of the shaft. The kick-starter arm itself is locked on to the outer splined length of shaft by means of a 10 mm pinch bolt.

Kick-starter motion is transferred to the engine through the quadrant engaging a bevel pinion on the rear of which are formed ratchet teeth engaging a bevel gear. This bevel gear mates with a bevel gear on the clutch unit which, in turn, engages with a bevel gear on the engine crankshaft. The three bevel gears are at right angles so that the starter pinion emerges in line with the engine crankshaft.

The clearance between the bevel gears is controlled by the thickness of the paper gasket between the cover plate and crankcase. It must therefore be replaced correctly. If the starter bevel is forced too far into mesh with the clutch bevel a whine will be noticeable when the engine is ticking over. The same effect is observed if the extended pinion shaft (150 c.c. models) is too tight a fit in its ball bearing. Either of these conditions can be checked by slackening off the cover plate slightly and observing the result. Permanent cure is effected by replacing or increasing the thickness of the paper gasket, or by reducing the extended pinion shaft diameter slightly by rubbing it down. The starter unit is assembled grease-packed for lubrication purposes. The presence of oil in the starter housing may be an indication that the gearbox has been overfilled or that the oil seal, a synthetic rubber ring on the starter bevel housing, has broken down.

6. CLUTCH

The clutch, Fig. 43, runs continually immersed in oil from the gearbox. It consists of three driven discs with rubber-cork friction material bonded to each face set alternately between two steel driving discs and a steel end plate and pressure plate. The driven discs are keyed to a splined collar on the shaft and the driving discs set in six grooves on the clutch-bell housing. Bevel gears drive the clutch bell. The splined collar and the gearbox main shaft connect together (*see* Fig. 46).

Driving and driven plates are pressed together by six springs, the pressure of which is relieved by operation of the clutch lever arm. This acts on the

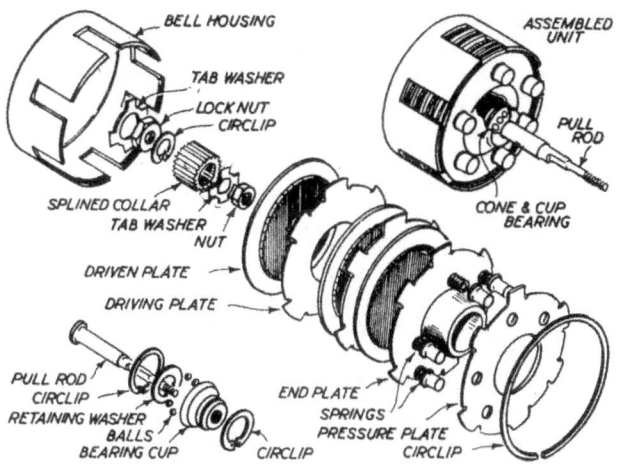

FIG. 43. EXPLODED AND ASSEMBLED VIEWS OF THE LAMBRETTA CLUTCH

end of a rod via a shouldered distance piece locked by two 8 mm nuts on the end of the rod. These nuts provide for clutch adjustment, being set so that the clutch begins to engage while there is still a small amount of free movement at the handlebar control lever. Free movement is increased by slackening off and re-tightening the 8 mm nuts near the end of the rod. To take up excess free movement these nuts must be tightened farther along the rod. The nuts are exposed by unscrewing the (19 mm) acorn nut protruding from the end of the clutch casing. If the clutch is adjusted too tightly, excessive wear may develop on the expanded cone end of the rod forming the cone and cup bearing which transmit movement of the rod into movement of the revolving clutch members. The cup section of this bearing thus rotates with the rotating clutch members while the cone (rod) does not rotate, the load being carried by ten $\frac{5}{32}$ in. ball bearings. Dismantling the clutch is usually necessary only when there is no further adjustment on the rod, or where such adjustment is no longer effective.

To dismantle the clutch completely, it is first necessary to take off the silencer and kick-starter cover plate assembly and starter pinion unit, (see p. 70). The brake linkage must also be detached when the rear brake is rod-operated.

The acorn nut is removed from the front of the clutch housing, followed by the two 8 mm nuts on the clutch rod. The clutch cable is then disconnected. The clutch housing is held in place with five Allen-head screws (5 mm key, jointed handle for ease of access) which when taken out enables the end cover to be removed. Some oil will escape from the gearbox when this is done and to save mess can be drawn off earlier by opening the drain and filler plugs.

A special clutch compressor tool is available which, when slipped over the clutch rod and tightened up sufficiently with one of the 8 mm nuts, will take up the load of the clutch springs enabling the large circlip to be removed. A suitable tool for this can be made at home, if necessary, from strip section iron at least $\frac{3}{32}$ in. thick and $\frac{1}{2}$ to 1 in. wide. After removing the circlip discs, cups and springs can be pulled out as a unit and dismantled further, as necessary.

If the pull rod is broken, or is suspected to be broken, the withdrawing tool will be ineffective. There is also the possibility that the balls in the cup and cone bearings may be lost and fall into the gearbox. Under such circumstances it is advisable to block off the back of the clutch with cloth and prise the circlip off with a screwdriver, then withdrawing the unit.

Wear on the friction discs can be estimated by measuring their overall thickness, stacked three together. This, however, is not always a reliable guide because the true wear or efficiency of the friction faces may be independent of physical thickness. Thus, it is possible for the cork constituent to be largely worn away from the cork-rubber compound which may have swelled slightly to give an apparently satisfactory thickness.

Data are: thickness, new, 15·5 mm (0·610 in.); limit of wear, 14 mm (0·551 in.). The springs are slightly stronger in 150 c.c. engines and extra-strong springs are normally fitted to machines converted to sidecar operation.

Discs are readily replaced, reassembly of the clutch reversing the above order. Where tab washers have been removed, these must be replaced and fitted properly, not left off altogether or replaced but not bent over properly. They should be replaced with new tab washers if the old ones break.

If further disassembly is required, the splined drum must be held in position with a special tool, or alternatively, unless the final drive has already been disassembled, by engaging top gear and putting on the rear brake this will hold the clutch centre from rotating. The 14 mm retaining nut can then be removed. This is a standard right-hand thread on 125 c.c. engines, but *left*-hand on 150 c.c. engines. The tab washer behind this nut should normally be replaced with a new one when refitting.

DETAILED MAINTENANCE AND ADJUSTMENT

The clutch centre is positioned with a very strong circlip on the shaft, and this is the next item to be removed. The hub of the clutch bell is held by a special spanner passed through the starter-drive pinion opening (removed in disassembling the kick-starter unit) and its fixing nut (24 mm) removed with a socket spanner. The bell is then extracted by mounting the special tool, i.e. inserting it into the bell, replacing the circlip which held the clutch discs and turning the extractor-tool screw against the end of the gearbox shaft. Behind the bell is a flange secured with three screws which, when removed, loosen the bevel bearing which is then ready to be withdrawn with the bevel pinion behind it when the gearbox has been

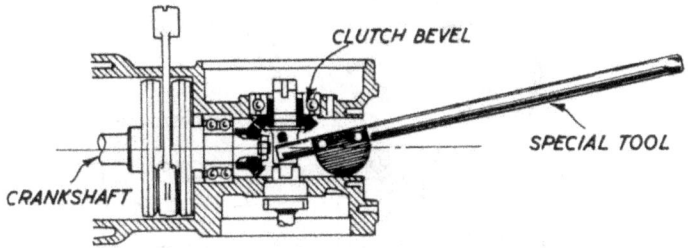

FIG. 44. A SPECIAL TOOL IS REQUIRED TO REMOVE THE CLUTCH BEVEL

dismantled and the shaft removed. A special puller tool, Fig. 44, is available simultaneously to free the pinion and sleeve.

7. TORSION BAR

Work on the gearbox, rear transmission and engine crankshaft or main bearing requires that the torsion-bar link be disconnected so that the engine unit may be pivoted forwards. It is often more convenient in major dismantling to remove the engine entirely from the machine. This can be done after first removing tank, engine cowling, carburettor, silencer and cables. The earth lead (black) should be disconnected from the screw on the back of the crankcase and the green and brown wires from the terminal block.

The rear wheel brake control and speedometer cables are detached and the rear wheel then removed. The front of the rear mudguard is freed by removing the two screws at the bottom and the two nuts and bolts at the top. The hydraulic damper, if fitted, should be disconnected. The torsion-bar link-pin must be taken out with the proper tool, Fig. 45, which enables the pin to be knocked out while at the same time it replaces it with a loose bush of the same diameter, but of the same thickness as the link so that the two can be separated. The simple type of pre-loading tool now available has an eccentric pin at the end and is an inexpensive item. It is, however, virtually impossible to knock out the link pin with a drift without damaging the caged rollers, and replacement of these is more costly than the special tool which guards against this possibility.

The engine is then held by its main pivot bolt secured with a nut and tab washer. When these are removed the engine can be lifted out of the frame. It may be necessary to knock out this pin but it should be done only with a soft hammer, or a block of wood, or soft metal. On older models, and all 125 c.c. engines utilizing bronze bushes instead of silent-blocks for mounting, the pin is of a different size and fitted with greasers. The greasers and caps are removed before the nut and washer, and a puller tool used to extract the pivot.

The rear suspension consists of the engine, gearbox, transmission and rear wheel as an integral unit swinging together about the frame pivot.

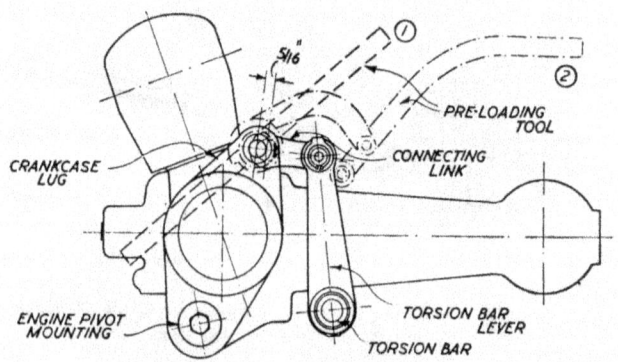

FIG 45. An Unloading Tool must be used to Release the Torsion-bar Connecting Link from the Crankcase Lugs

The old pattern tool is shown at (2). The latest tool (1) is a British design and does the same job more simply. The roller cage will be damaged if the pin is driven out without the special tool.

This swing is controlled by linking the engine group to the torsion-bar return lever on the upper portion of the crankcase on the flywheel side. The torsion bar itself is fully enclosed in a seating welded to the bottom of the frame, and locked at one end.

Any "swing" loading is therefore transferred to the torsion bar in the form of "twist," the specification of the material being such that static and dynamic torsion are absorbed at an even rate. The required degree of preloading is achieved by having 22 splines at one end of the torsion bar and 21 splines at the other, thus making possible a vernier adjustment. Limit stops for extreme displacement of the engine are provided in the form of two rubber buffers attached to lugs, one on the crankcase and one on the frame. The condition of these buffers should be checked if the engine is removed, and they should be replaced if damaged.

A roller bearing is incorporated in the upper shackle joint, lubricated with grease via a nipple. A grease point is also fitted to the bottom of the seating (casing), this being maintained as a grease-packed unit. Lack of

DETAILED MAINTENANCE AND ADJUSTMENT   77

attention to lubrication at this point may result in excessive wear or even seizure of the torsion bar. Similarly, damage to the assembly may result if the shackle hole becomes worn. There should be no play in these bearings when assembled.

The torsion bar is positioned with the 22 splines engaging the fixed part of the frame, and the 21 splines engaging the torsion-bar lever arm. When offered to the crankcase lugs there should be one-half a hole distance or $\frac{5}{16}$ in. separating the two holes if the preloading on the torsion bar is

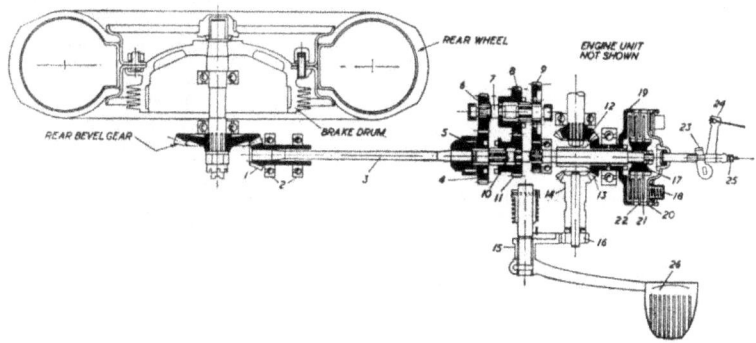

FIG. 46. CLUTCH, GEARBOX AND REAR DRIVE ASSEMBLY ON D AND LD MODELS

Key

1. Rear bevel pinion.
2. Ball-races.
3. Transmission shaft.
4. Output pinion.
5. Needle-roller bearing.
6. Keyed gear on layshaft.
7. Layshaft.
8. Second gear on layshaft.
9. Neutral gear on layshaft.
10. Main shaft.
11. Second gear on main shaft.
12. Crankshaft bevel pinion.
13. Clutch bevel gear.
14. Kick-starter bevel pinion.
15. Kick-starter notched sector.
16. Starter pinion gear.
17. Clutch splined collar.
18. Clutch spring.
19. Clutch bell.
20. Clutch end-plate.
21. Clutch-driven discs.
22. Clutch-driving discs.
23–24. Clutch-lever assembly.
25. Clutch adjusting nuts.
26. Kick-starter pedal.

correct. It is permissible to increase this slightly, if required, by resetting the torsion bar and/or lever arm. A special tool is used to apply preloading to the torsion bar and to align the shackle end with the crankcase lugs to insert the pin. This is lightly punched in place and locked with the safety ring and circlip.

8. GEARBOX

(Figs. 46 and 47. *See also* Fig. 15)

With the torsion bar linkage detached and the engine pivoted forwards, or removed from the frame ready access is available to the bottom screws holding the transmission case to the crankcase. If the engine is still pivoted to the frame the rear mudguard should also be removed at this stage. The gear selector cover is readily detached by removing the three screws holding it in place and unspringing the circlip from the selector spindle. Expose the three screws holding the selector box by engaging in first gear, then undo the screws and remove the selector box complete.

The transmission case is secured to the crankcase by six Allen screws (5 mm), four 6 mm screws and one 12 mm screw; also a 14 mm nut and bolt at the extreme bottom, this being an alignment bolt. All have one

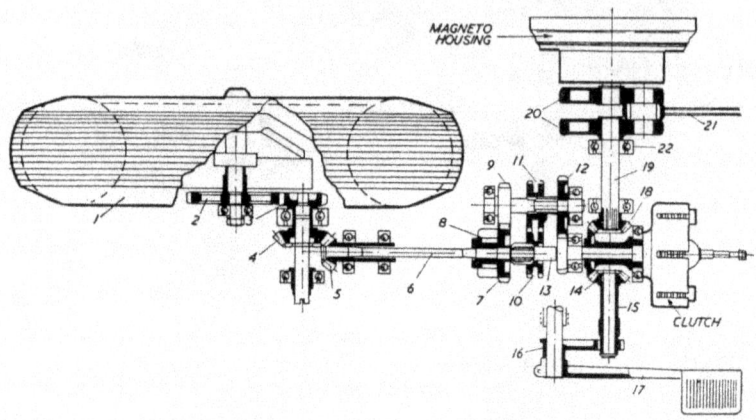

FIG. 47. MAIN DIFFERENCES BETWEEN THE TRANSMISSION ON MODELS B, C, AND LC, SHOWN HERE, ARE CLEAR BY COMPARISON WITH FIG. 46

Key

1. Rear wheel.
2. Large reduction gear.
3. Small reduction gear.
4. Bevel pinion.
5. Bevel pinion.
6. Transmission shaft.
7. Output pinion.
8. Needle roller bearing.
9. Keyed gear on layshaft.
10. Selector gear (mainshaft).
11. Selector gear (layshaft).
12. Neutral gear on layshaft.
13. Main shaft.
14. Kick-starter bevel mating with clutch bevel.
15. Kick-starter pinion.
16. Kick-starter unit.
17. Kick-starter pedal arm.
18. Crankshaft bevel.
19. Crankshaft.
20. Crankshaft webs.
21. Connecting rod.
22. Crankshaft bearing.

plain and one spring washer under the heads. Once the transmission case is withdrawn the gearbox layshaft will fall free and all gears can readily be pulled out. It is possible to reassemble the layshaft and sliding gears so that the operation of the selector arm and eccentric adjustment can be checked.

Points to look for are signs of wear or damage, calling for replacement, on any gear tooth and the depth of engagement achieved in each gear. The eccentric acts as a fulcrum pin for a pawl spring loaded to fall into the notches on the selector gate, thus locating the gear positions. The

DETAILED MAINTENANCE AND ADJUSTMENT

eccentric is located by two 8 mm bolts and is adjusted by means of the oil-plug tool which fits into the hexagonal hole of the disc below the selector box on the transmission casing.

Full mesh in top gear is obtained when the eccentric is in the position giving the greatest clockwise (angular) movement of the gear selector arm. Full mesh in first gear is obtained by the *opposite* adjustment. Thus adjustment of the depth of mesh of one of these gears can be obtained only at the expense of the other.

If full engagement cannot be obtained it is permissible to grind down the third gear notch to a maximum of 1 mm. For this purpose the selector gate is removed by withdrawing the selector spindle. It is important that if this notch is deepened, the same *form* should be preserved.

Gearbox reassembly should be fairly logical, all the gears being mounted in the transmission case before replacing this on the crankshaft. It is important that the two plain washers should be replaced one on each end of the layshaft and that all gears mesh perfectly before finally tightening up the transmission case. Operation of the gears can be checked by turning the engine over by hand, operating the gear shift and checking that the drive is in order. It will be found when replacing the selector arm on the splined end of the selector spindle that only one position will enable all three gears to be obtained.

9. FINAL DRIVE (Fig. 48)

The transmission shaft and rear drive is removable as a unit, following the instruction given in Section 8. It is not necessary that either the clutch or kick-starter mechanism be removed if only this unit is to receive attention.

The stub axle forms a unit with the crown wheel and bearing, bolted to the transmission casing with four 14 mm nuts, the fulcrum pin of the brake shoes, which has two flats to enable it to be unscrewed from the casing, and the hollow sleeve containing the cam spindle for the rear brake operation. This sleeve is held by a 24 mm nut and is removed together with the backplate. (*See* Chapter IV, and Section 3 of this chapter for details of dismantling the rear wheel, if in difficulties on this point.)

The crown wheel can be dismantled from the stub axle by temporarily refitting the rear wheel to hold the axle against rotation, and undoing the 19 mm nut. The housing for the wheel bearing serves also to prevent sideways movement of the axle and is held to the backplate with four 10 mm nuts. An oil seal is held in this housing with a spring circlip, and a small rubber ring is fitted at the back of the housing for a similar purpose. Both seals must be in good condition to exclude all oil from inside the rear hub, since this will affect the efficiency of the brakes. Where such trouble persists, in spite of apparently good seals, the advice of a servicing agent should be sought as it is possible the cause may be due to a positive

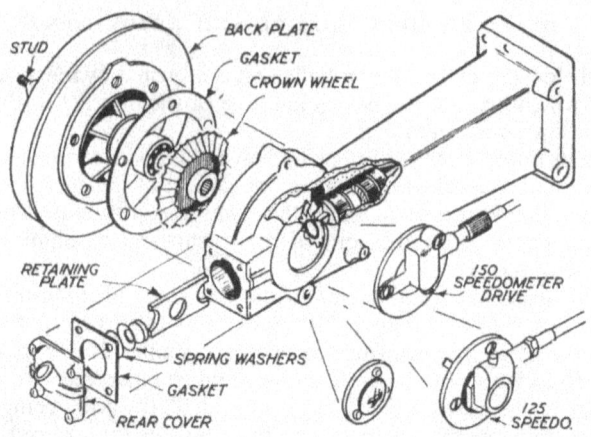

Fig. 48 (*a*). Diagram of the Rear Transmission Assembly

Speedometer-drive units differ on the 125 c.c. and 150 c.c. models, as shown. Where no speedo is fitted a plain cover is standard.

Fig. 48 (*b*). General View of Standard 150 c.c. LD Model

A is a breather fitted to the transmission case to prevent pressure build-up forcing oil past seals into rear hub. *B* is speedo drive; *C* rear-brake clamp plates joining brake arm; *D* gear selector; *E* air filter on carburettor; *F* kick-starter pedal (shapes have differed on various models); *G* footbrake pedal.

pressure build-up in the transmission case and gearbox. Some later models have a special vent on the top of the transmission case to overcome this.

The bevel pinion is assembled as a group together with its two ball bearings and an oil seal. This group is pressed in place in the machined recess in the transmission case. A special tool is required to extract this group. It can, however, be driven out, with a large diameter drift or punch, from the gearbox end of the casing. The punch must straddle the unit, otherwise the aluminium end cap will be damaged. The end cover of the crankcase unit, which carries the filler plug and oil level plug, is held in position with four screws and can be detached together with the cone washers, spacing disc and retaining plate, this assembly transmitting spring

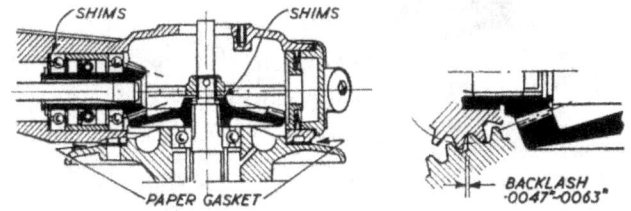

FIG. 49. CLEARANCE BETWEEN REAR BEVELS SHOULD BE HELD TO LIMITS SHOWN FOR QUIET OPERATION
Adjustable by shims and paper gasket.

pressure to the pinion bearings. The cone washers must always be assembled back-to-back, i.e. the larger diameters outwards, in order to obtain the correct spring pressure.

Clearance between crown wheel and pinion is governed by the thickness of the paper gasket between the backplate and transmission case, Fig. 49. There should normally be between 0·002 and 0·004 in. clearance between crown wheel and pinion-tooth faces.

The transmission shaft itself is relatively small in diameter this being a deliberate feature of the design to achieve flexibility in torsion and thus absorb shock loads in the transmission. It engages with the pinion by means of a splined end. Both ends of the transmission shaft are splined in a similar manner, the other end to engage the driving gear from the gearbox, and this shaft may be replaced either way round. With the pinion assembly fitted in the transmission casing the shaft can be offered and turned to engage the splines, if completely withdrawn.

Two types of speedometer are fitted. The 125 c.c. machines are fitted with a Smith speedometer unit as standard in which the worm and drive to the cable are integral with the housing unit. Only a spade-shaped shaft protrudes inwards, engaging with a slot in the end of the rear axle shaft, when assembled. 150 c.c. machines are fitted with a Veglia speedometer unit, which is slightly different in appearance. Only the worm unit is

82   THE BOOK OF THE LAMBRETTA MOTOR-SCOOTER

actually integral with the casing unit, mounted on the end of the speedometer cable, and a drive pinion is fitted over the end of the rear axle and locked to it with a pin. This drive pinion remains on the axle if the speedometer casing is unscrewed and removed.

10. MAGNETO UNIT (Figs 50, 51 and 52)

All models have a similar type of flywheel magneto, either Filso or Marelli. Later models of either type incorporate an automatic ignition advance

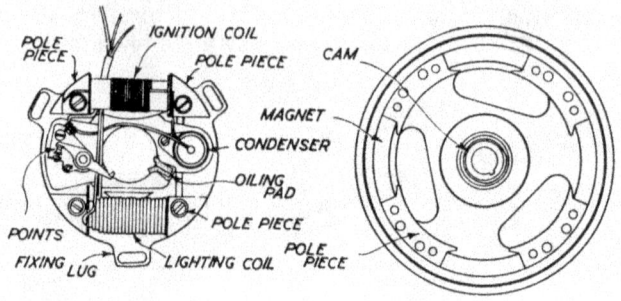

Fig. 50. Filso Flywheel Magneto for 150 c.c. Machines with Separate Ignition Coil

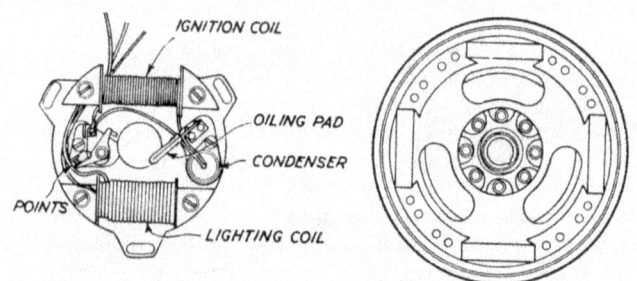

Fig. 51. Marelli Flywheel Magneto is Alternative for 150 c.c. Models

It is essentially similar to the Filso pattern.

mechanism. The high-tension coils on both types are interchangeable (150 c.c. machines) and both are identical for fitting to the crankcase. Electric starter machines (LDA) have a somewhat modified unit with more powerful magnets. It is therefore important to specify the make of Magneto and model when ordering replacement parts. The electrical side of the magneto system is discussed in detail in Chapter VII and the mechanical aspects only will be considered here. Normally the only part requiring attention should be the contact breaker although the whole

DETAILED MAINTENANCE AND ADJUSTMENT   83

magneto unit has to be removed to gain access to the engine for removal of the crankshaft or main bearings.

The interior of the flywheel magneto is exposed by removing the conical cover, held by a spring clip. This gives access to the contact breaker unit for cleaning and adjusting the points. The gap can be adjusted by slackening off the locking screw next to the contacts and moving the fixed point, e.g. prising with a screwdriver, or by turning a small eccentric screw adjacent to the locking screw; on some models only. The contact points should also be inspected. They should be clean, smooth and flat. If necessary remove them entirely and file or grind. The contact breaker gap maximum

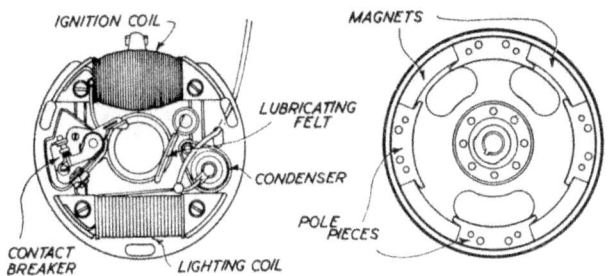

FIG. 52. FILSO MAGNETO AS FITTED TO 125 C.C. MACHINES
The high-tension coil incorporates a secondary winding connected directly to the spark plug, hence no external coil is employed.

opening should be about 0·016 to 0·020 in. although this is dependent on the timing setting. Timing can be checked by referring to Chapter VII.

To remove the flywheel it is necessary to lock it against rotation—a special tool is available for holding the flywheel—and to unscrew the 19 mm nut holding it on the crankshaft. The flywheel should not be locked by jamming something against the cast in fins on the periphery, as these may be damaged or broken by such action. Once the nut is removed the flywheel is removed from the shaft with a special puller in preference to prising off.

This exposes the stator plate with attached coils and contact breaker unit. If the main leads are disconnected the stator plate can be freed from its housing by releasing the three screws.

The automatic advance and retard mechanism incorporated on later models differs for the Marelli and Filso magnetos. In the Marelli unit, on left in Fig. 53, a single expansion weight and arm is used, and the Filso unit, on right in Fig. 53, incorporates two swinging plates with bobweights attached interconnected by a coil spring. One of the main differences from a maintenance point of view is that with the Filso unit the plates cover the 19 mm flywheel retaining nut and so have to be separated by removal of the spring before this nut can be reached. A further point to note is that the white ring (plastic) is fitted to act as a "silent" stop for the weights when they expand and should be removed before any locking tool is inserted to remove the unit, otherwise the plastic will be damaged. The regulating mechanism itself should not require any adjustment on either model although in the Marelli unit it is sometimes an improvement to shorten the spring by two or three coils. This will prevent premature opening which does sometimes occur with a fairly fast tick-over and which is evidenced by a rattle in the flywheel unit.

The action of the mechanism is basically the same in both cases. With increasing speed the bob weight (or weights) tends to rotate the carrying

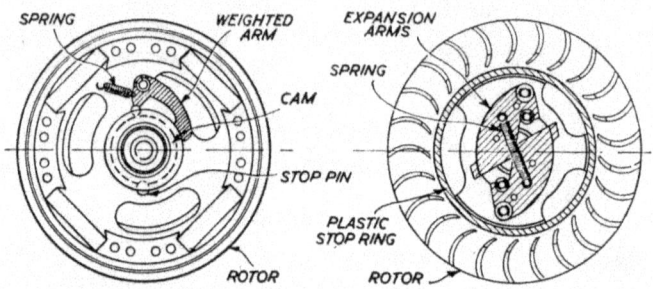

FIG. 53. AUTOMATIC ADVANCE AND RETARD MECHANISMS ARE INCORPORATED ON LATER MAGNETOS

Marelli unit (*left*) has a single weighted arm. The Filso unit (*right*) has two expanding plates and a plastic "stop" ring.

plate(s) outwards. This movement is transferred to the cam which opens the contact breaker points and so advances the point of opening with increasing engine speed. Timing adjustment must always be made with the advance mechanism fully expanded.

11. CRANKSHAFT AND PISTON ASSEMBLY (Fig. 54)

Cylinder head and barrel and flywheel and stator must first be removed; also the kick-starter mechanism and clutch assembly on the right side of the engine (*see* the respective Sections). The crankshaft nut on the magneto side is 27 mm, locked by a tab washer. The tabs must be straightened, e.g. with a screwdriver, before attempting to undo the nut, and the washer replaced if damaged. The crankshaft must also be locked against rotation. This can be done with a special tool or a piece of wood inserted through the cylinder opening. Remove circlips, oil seal and distance piece and small rubber ring.

The magneto flange, held by six 10 mm bolts, is removed next. The flange must be withdrawn with a special extractor. It is sealed against the crankcase with a rubber ring. Remaining on the shaft will be a spacing washer and a second oil seal located by a circlip. It should be noted that the two oil seals face with their open ends towards the crankcase.

Assembly is slightly different on 125 c.c. engine which have two separate ball races instead of the single (double row) bearing, separated by a distance piece and only one oil seal. In both types the main bearings on this side of the engine are a tight fit in the magneto flange and if they have to be removed the housing must be expanded with heat, e.g. boiling water.

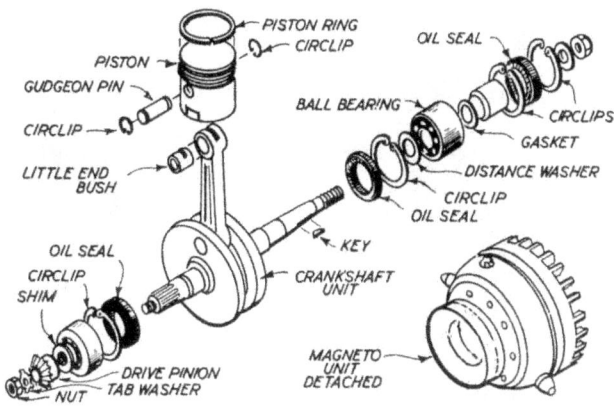

FIG. 54. CRANKSHAFT ASSEMBLY OF THE 150 C.C. ENGINE

The crankshaft itself and connecting rod is a factory-assembled unit. The 125 c.c. crankshaft can be disassembled and assembly also differs in other small details.

Similarly, the housing must be expanded before a replacement bearing can be refitted.

At the gearbox side of the crankshaft the bevel-drive pinion is accessible with clutch, kick-starter assemblies and gear shaft removed. The crankshaft bevel pinion is locked on the shaft with a *left-hand* nut (17 mm) locked with a tab washer. When this is removed the shaft may be drifted towards the magneto side which will withdraw the shaft from the bevel pinion and free it. It can then be worked out of the crankcase on the magneto side, complete with connecting rod.

The two-piece crankshaft is assembled as a factory unit complete with connecting rod and big-end bearing on all 150 c.c. models. It is made as a separable unit on 125 c.c. engines. Earlier versions of the 150 c.c. engine have connecting rods with 14 mm small-end bushes. Replacement units are available with 16 mm small ends only. Hence when replacing an original shaft with the smaller size of small end on the connecting rod it will also be necessary to replace the piston and gudgeon pin assembly to match the replacement shaft assembly.

The most vital part in the reassembly of the engine is obtaining the right degree of mesh between the crankshaft bevel gear and the clutch bevel. This, in fact, is the only feature of the Lambretta where careful matching is essential, if engine whine is to be eliminated. Steel shims are employed to space the respective bevels away from their bearing faces and are available in a variety of thicknesses, Fig. 55. A certain amount of experience is necessary to judge when the correct degree of mesh has been obtained, assembling the clutch bell, and rotating it together with the crankshaft

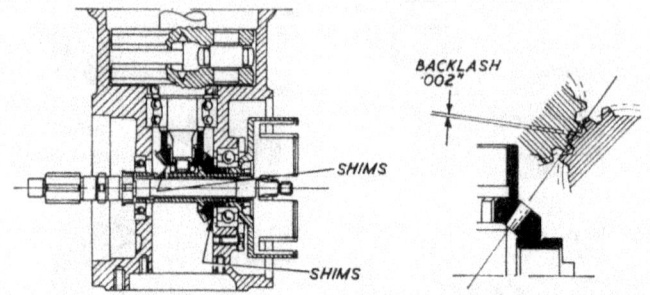

FIG. 55. BACKLASH BETWEEN THE CRANKSHAFT BEVEL AND CLUTCH BEVEL SHOULD NOT EXCEED 0·002 in.

Setting up these two gears is the only tricky part in reassembling the Lambretta engine.

bevel by hand. Provided the bevels are smooth and free from independent movement the engagement should give quiet running.

12. CARBURETTOR (Figs. 56 and 57)

A Dell'Orto carburettor is standard on all Lambrettas, the type number varying somewhat according to the age of the machine. This, for the most part, affects only the size of the standard jets and needle. A Zenith MCT 19 carburettor is fitted to some 125 c.c. engines. The carburettor model should be checked when ordering replacements as, in addition to calibration, some of the major components may not be interchangeable, e.g. carburettor body and float.

Maintenance is largely a matter of adjustment and correction for needle and atomizer wear. Idling adjustment is done via the throttle control and mixture screws, Fig. 57. These adjustments should be made with the engine warm. The throttle control screw is adjusted first, and with the engine running slowly finer adjustments made by means of the (horizontal) mixture screw. Unscrewing this screw weakens the mixture and will tend to make the engine slow up, or stop. Screwing in will richen the mixture and tend to make the engine speed up. The correct adjustment is one which gives the slowest, even running equivalent to an engine crankshaft speed of 1,000 to 1,500 r.p.m. when idling. It cannot be expected, however, that

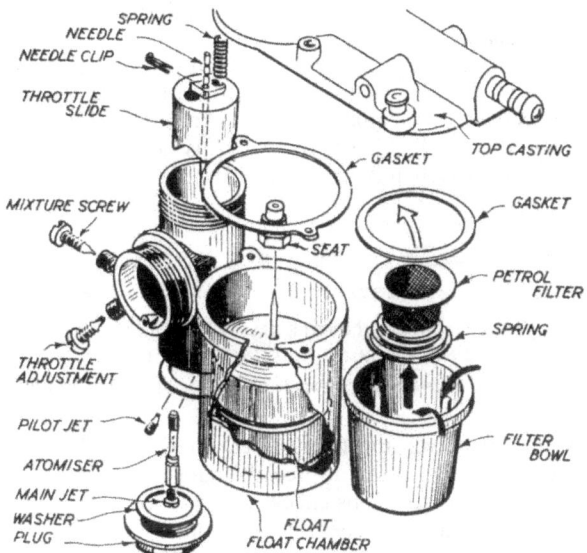

Fig. 56. Dell'Orto Carburettor as used on the 125 c.c. Engines shown in Exploded Detail

Petrol flows down into the filter bowl and then up through the gauze filter.

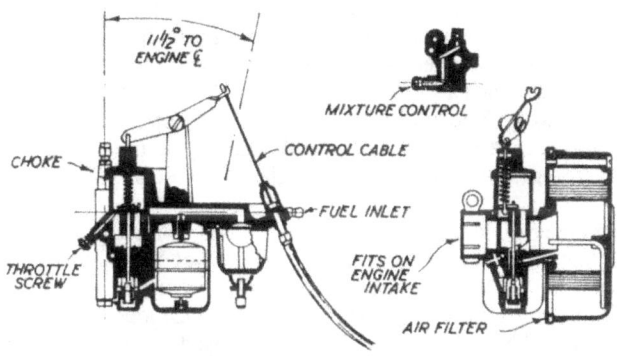

Fig. 57. The Dell'Orto Carburettor for 150 c.c. Engines shown in Section

A conventional choke unit is incorporated. Adjustment is by the mixture and throttle screws shown.

a single-cylinder two-stroke engine can be adjusted to idle as smoothly and as quietly as a multi-cylinder car engine.

The starter device is merely a choke which provides a by-pass path for the mixture, and it is most effective when the throttle is fully closed. It supplies an excessively-rich mixture to the induction pipe for ease of starting when the engine is cold. Unless the choke is depressed when the engine is running, an over-rich mixture will continue to be fed to the engine,

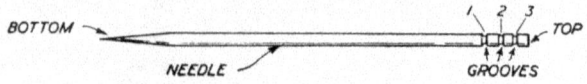

Fig. 58. The Throttle Needle has Three Grooves or Ridges near the Top End. Normal Setting is in the Second Groove
Compensation for wear may be made by moving up to the third groove.

resulting in loss of power and throttle response, as well as increasing the rate of fuel consumption by an appreciable amount.

If faulty carburation develops check—

(i) **Air Filter.** If this becomes blocked the supply of air to the carburettor will be reduced, resulting in the mixture being affected (too rich). Regular cleaning out with petrol is good practice.

(ii) **Float.** This may have become damaged or developed a leak, or be incorrectly placed on the needle. If the needle is not in properly, round end first, the clip may damage the needle point. If the float needle point is damaged or worn it will not seal properly and lead to flooding. Flooding may also be caused by dirt which has filtered into the bottom of the float chamber or around the needle seating. Periodic cleaning is recommended. Flooding can also be caused by excessive engine vibration.

(iii) **Air Leaks.** The fuel line should be a tight fit over both the carburettor and fuel tap. Air leakage will weaken the mixture and cause the engine to run unduly hot. Check that the carburettor gaskets are in good order.

(iv) **Atomizer.** The hole in the atomizer will gradually enlarge and will pay for checking every 5,000 miles. It should not be necessary to think of replacement before this age, and not normally before 10,000 miles or more. If the hole is enlarged, replace with a standard-size jet.

(v) **Needle.** The main needle is also subject to wear. It should be adjusted progressively to compensate for wear by shifting the clip at the top so that the needle advances another notch, Fig. 58. A suitable interval for adjustment is 5,000 miles.

(vi) **Main and Idling Jets.** Apart from cleaning, these can be checked at about the same interval as the needle, and replaced if necessary.

(vii) **Throttle Valve.** This should not normally give any trouble but if tight or sticky could affect idling performance.

DETAILED MAINTENANCE AND ADJUSTMENT 89

Carburettor Data
125 c.c. Engines

	Type	Throttle valve	Needle	Needle posn.	Atomizer	Jets Main	Min.	Idler screw Min.
Dell'Orto	MA18B2	N50	ND1	groove 2	N260B	0·0295 in.	0·0157 in.	1 turn
,,	MA18B3	N75	ND1	groove 2	N255B	0·0157 in.	0·0177 in.	1 turn
Zenith	MCT19					100/100 mm	—	—

150 c.c. Engines

	Type	Throttle valve	Needle	Needle posn.	Atomizer	Jets Main	Needle	Starter
Dell'Orto	MA19B4	N75	D3	groove 2	255B	72	40	No 50 (engine nos. prior to 8200) No. 75 (engine nos. from 8201)

13. FRONT FORKS (Fig. 59)

The handlebar assembly differs slightly on various models but the attention required to this end of the machine is usually limited to periodic (5,000 mile interval) tightening of the steering bearings. If, however, the forks have been bent, the front fork assembly will need to be removed for straightening or replacement. If this condition is suspected, e.g. after an accident, a rough check can be made by sighting the front wheel with the handlebars straight. Mis-alignment is most easily spotted by sighting from the rear of the machine against the back wheel. To check if the forks have been bent back, see if a hand can be slipped between the rear of the front mudguard and the front tube of the frame. There should normally be three-quarters of an inch clearance here.

The centre of the handlebars is straddled by a support which in turn is locked to the steering column with a nut and bolt and one plain and one spring washer. If these are removed the handlebars can be lifted off the steering column. The front brake cable should preferably be disconnected before doing this. On later machines this bolt is also part of the parking lock and when refitted must only be tightened up with the handlebars turned to the locked position.

Removal of the handlebars exposes the two ring nuts locking the steering head ball races. These are of cycle type, the upper race containing thirty-six $\frac{1}{8}$ in. diameter balls and the lower race, at the bottom of the tube, twenty-three $\frac{1}{4}$ in. balls. Adjustment is by tightening or slackening the ring nuts, the second ring nut acting as a lock for the first when tightened right up against it. If the ring nuts are removed the top race assembly can be withdrawn and the front forks pulled out through the frame tube. The lower race components can then be withdrawn. The cone will, of course, have to be driven off. It is necessary to remove the forks in this manner only for repairs to the forks, or to remove the front mudguard in which case it is not necessary to remove the bottom bearing cone from its seat. If the forks are to be returned for repair, all components should be stripped off. This entails removing the front wheel complete. The suspension box covers are then removed by undoing the three (8 mm) screws and driving them through roughly 90 degrees; they will not come off until the inner faces are exposed. They can then be levered or tapped off together with the bush which forms the bearing of the suspension link arm. The pinch bolt can now be slackened on the splined spindle and the lever sprung away from the spring cup. Removal of the bottom buffer

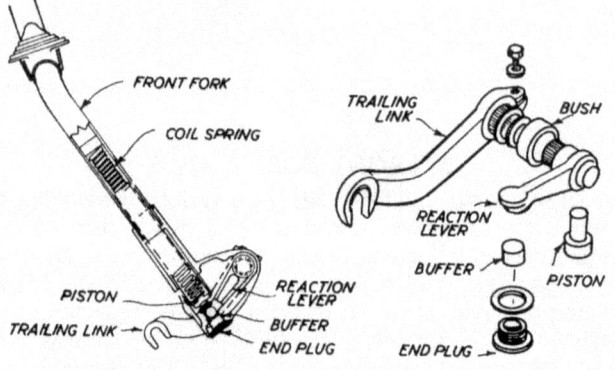

FIG. 59. DETAILS OF THE FRONT SUSPENSION ON D AND LD MODELS

The coil springs must be replaced the right way round—closer coils towards the top. Reaction lever operates against spring through a piston. Down movement is buffered by a rubber stop.

block then enables the spring to be withdrawn from the tube. The same operation is repeated for the other side.

To reassemble it is best to grip the steering column in a vice, supported horizontally. The spring is well greased and inserted with the closer coils towards the top of the tube. A special tool is made for preloading the springs and push block so that the inner lever can be assembled in the suspension box with its roller end resting against the push block at the bottom of the spring.

14. SELF-STARTER (Figs. 60 and 61)

The LDA model incorporates a self-starter motor as a separate unit bolted to the front of a modified clutch cover. Position of the starter motor is immediately above the silencer, which unit is of the later types shown in Figs. 39 and 40. The starter motor unit is held on to the clutch cover by two long Allen screws (5 mm) which extend through to the crankcase, and a shorter screw from the clutch cover into the motor. The starter switch is fitted to the motor casing by two 8 mm nuts. Sandwiched between is a rubber washer. A rubber grommet seals the entry of the leads to the switch. The electric motor is a sealed unit, as far as lubrication is concerned

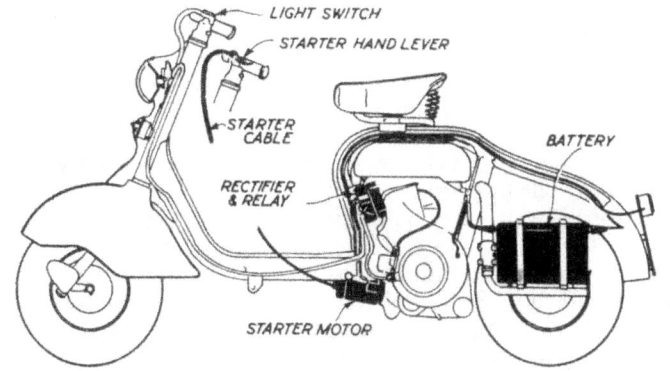

Fig. 60. Disposition of the Special Components on the 125 c.c. LDA Self-starter Model

On LDB models (without self-starter) the rectifier for charging is in the same place.

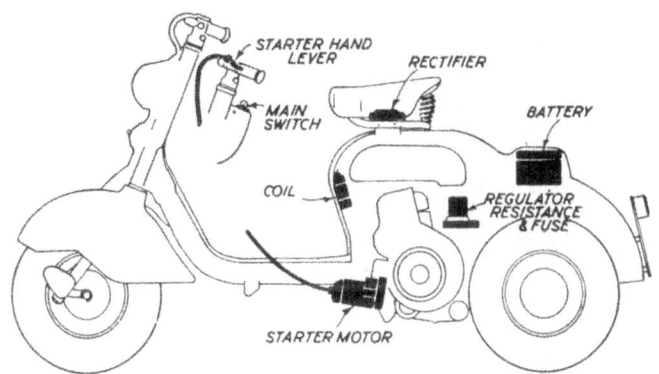

Fig. 61. The 150 c.c. 12-volt LDA Self-starter Model

On all self-starter machines the starter motor is operated by a handlebar lever The 150 c.c. LDA model has a car-type ignition switch on dash panel and dispenses with the normal light switch on handlebars.

and thus has no lubricating points. The reduction gear unit is grease packed and rubber-ring oil-seals are fitted to exclude oil which might otherwise be transferred from the clutch.

The motor drives a floating pinion mounted on a countershaft via a pair of reduction gears, the countershaft remaining in constant engagement with the motor. The countershaft is hollow, and traversing the centre is a rod controlling the sliding movement of the starter pinion. The pinion is pushed along the counter shaft to engage with teeth set on the outside of the clutch bell as soon as the electric motor begins to turn, thus engaging the starter motor with the engine. Sliding movement is by a spring compressed when the pinion teeth are opposite the clutch teeth. A freewheel device is also incorporated in the pinion so that the electric motor cannot be turned by the engine.

Normally this unit should not be subject to any maintenance or adjustment requirements. It may, however, be necessary to remove the motor (taking off the silencer first) in order to get at the switch and clean off corrosion or oil which may have affected the contacts; or to replace the brushes on the motor after a considerable period of wear. Faults which may occur will nearly always be concerned with the electrical circuitry which is described in the next chapter. Self-starter machines operate on a 12-volt a.c./d.c. system, as opposed to the 6-volt a.c. system on standard machines, and the circuitry is considerably different.

It is interesting to note that the load imposed by the starter motor is far less severe on the battery than in a normal motor-car system. The battery is of 13 amp-hr capacity and maximum demand from the starter is 30 amps. On a normal motor-car system although the battery capacity may be four or five times as great, starter motor consumption is usually six or seven times as great. However, the motor demand is still relatively high for any battery and thus excessive use of the starter motor will tend to run the battery down quickly. This will normally be compensated for by the fact that the battery is recharged continuously with the engine running. Thus it is important to see that the charging system continues to function properly.

Chief misuse of the starter is in running it for excessively long periods in starting up. A maximum time of five seconds should be adequate for starting in even the coldest weather. A longer period is an indication of mis-adjustment of the starting controls, or a fault. The kick-starter unit is still retained on the 150 c.c. self-starter machines and so failure of the starter merely means reverting to foot starting. Failure of the starter motor will most likely be due to a run down battery or dirty motor switch. The starter is powerful enough to turn the engine over rapidly even in the coldest weather and so no difficulty should be experienced in this respect. If, however, the battery is low and the starter sluggish on a very cold morning, especially if the machine has been idle for a week or so, freeing the engine by kicking over the engine with the kick-starter first is good practice.

Component positions of a typical 125 c.c. self-starter model and a 150 c.c. self-starter model are shown in Figs. 60 and 61, respectively, although the coil positions may be found to vary on different models. Wiring diagrams are given in Chapter VII.

CHAPTER VII

IGNITION AND LIGHTING

POWER FOR IGNITION on all models is supplied by a flywheel magneto. Main differences are that on 125 c.c. machines the high tension, to the plug, is extracted direct from the magneto unit, but on 150 c.c. machines the magneto current is fed to a separate high-tension coil mounted on the frame of the machine. Current in both cases is produced by the ignition coil of the magneto. The magneto also generates a low-voltage alternating current through a second coil, the lighting coil, which feeds the lighting circuit, incorporating the horn. Thus, the engine supplies electrical power for lighting all the time the engine is running.

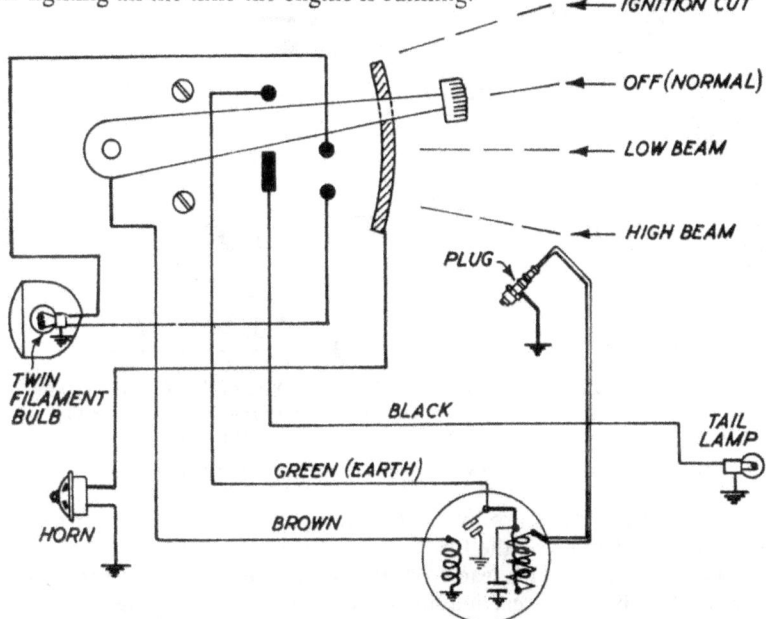

FIG. 62. STANDARD WIRING DIAGRAM FOR 125 C.C. D AND LD MODELS
Most have horn button integral with handlebar switch; operated by downward pressure.

ELECTRICAL CIRCUITS

Basic electrical circuits for the 125 c.c. and 150 c.c. engines are shown in Figs. 62 and 63, respectively. Fig. 63 also incorporates a pilot light for night driving without using the headlight, and a bulb light for the speedometer. These refinements are standard fitting on later machines.

Parking lights are also provided on later models or can be adapted on earlier machines, by incorporating a small 6-volt accumulator in the circuit. It is not, however, possible to adapt old machines to battery lighting since there is no suitable pick-up lead on the lighting coil of the magneto. The lighting coil must, therefore, be replaced with one of later

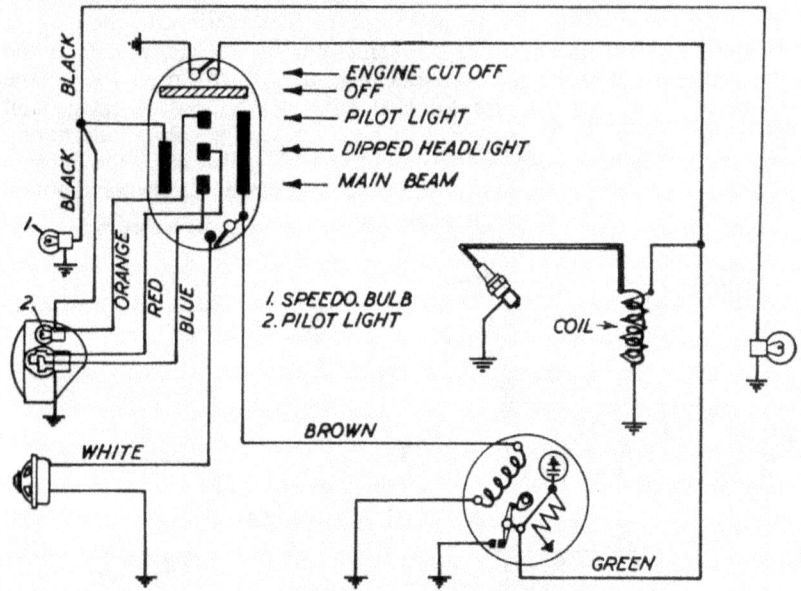

Fig. 63. Standard Wiring Diagram for 150 c.c. Machines, Introducing Pilot Light in Headlamp on Separate Switch Position and Speedometer Bulb (optional)

The horn switch is a separate button on the handlebar switch unit.

type, with an earth return by a soldered wire to the pole-piece of the coil, the red lead then being the feed wire to the rectifier. The red lead on the old type coil is the earth lead from the coil and is earthed on the terminal block. This battery is carried immediately behind the engine. To replace energy drawn from the battery using the parking lights, a rectifier is coupled to the lighting coil to provide a charge for the battery when the engine is running. The complete wiring diagram is then as in Fig. 64. The fuse and rectifier are contained in a small case attached to the frame of the machine immediately below and in front of the tank on LD models. The arrangement is slightly different on D models although the circuit connexions are identical.

IGNITION AND LIGHTING

The charging circuit can readily be checked by connecting an ammeter in the main battery lead, i.e. by disconnecting the lead from the positive terminal of the battery and connecting up again through an ammeter—ammeter negative terminal to battery positive. With the main switch lever to the "off" position and with the engine running, charging current should be indicated on the ammeter, varying from about 0·2 amps at fast idling speed up to a maximum of 0·9 amps wtih the engine running fast, about 5,000 r.p.m. For specific measurement of engine speed the

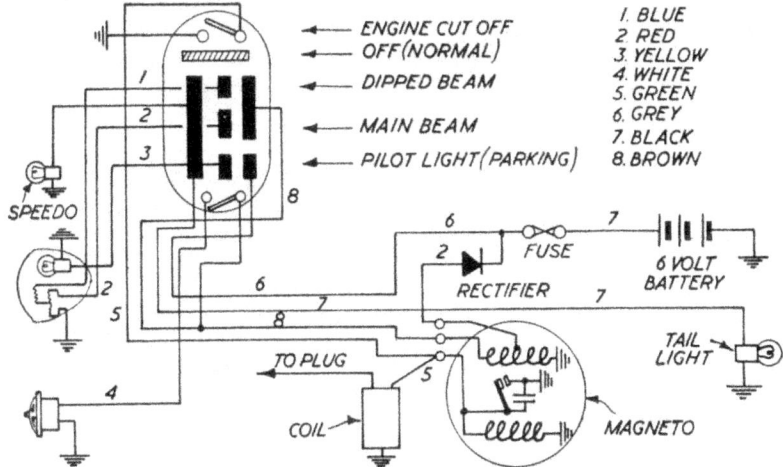

Fig. 64. Standard Wiring Diagram for LDB (battery parking light) Models

Connexions and leads may readily be identified by the colour coding employed. Rectifier and coil are usually mounted close together on the machine, but sometimes coil is on rear of frame (r.h. side).

flywheel cover can be detached and a tachometer held against the flywheel lock nut, when specified charging rates are—

at 3,000 r.p.m. engine speed—0·4 amps
at 5,000 r.p.m. engine speed—0·9 amps

(*Note:* 30 m.p.h. in top gear is equivalent to an engine speed of 3,000 r.p.m.)

No-charge may be due to a burnt out fuse, in which case the parking lights will be inoperative when switched on. A weak charge may be due to failure of the magneto, de-magnetization, or a faulty rectifier. Magneto failure can be identified from the fact that the headlight will be weak with the engine running, although the headlight will also be weak if the wires are connected wrongly to the magneto socket, e.g. replaced the wrong way round after removing the magneto unit. Correct connexion is best identified by reference to the colour code in the wiring diagram.

A continually-failing battery, e.g. parking lights weak, may be due to poor recharging, which can be checked as above, or to excessive electrical leak. The rectifier is essentially a one-way electrical switch although it will pass a very small current continuously in the opposite direction. This can be checked with a *milliammeter* and should not exceed 3 milliamps in value; engine not running and lighting switch "off." A higher value than this indicates either a faulty rectifier or a partial "short" in the wiring due to bared or frayed leads.

Excessive use of the parking lights will, of course, discharge the battery beyond the recovery achieved when running. The capacity of the battery

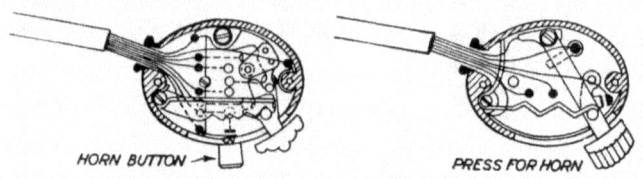

FIG. 65. TWO TYPES OF SWITCH AS USED ON 125 C.C. MACHINES

The one on the left is typical of a 125 c.c. model with battery lighting and regulator-type charging. The right-hand switch is standard for D and LD 125 c.c. machines.

when fully charged is such as to give approximately two hours continuous lighting without recharging. When parking lights have to be used excessively it may be necessary to remove and recharge the battery at intervals to keep it in good condition. The battery should never be left to discharge completely or left in a discharged state, even if the parking lights are not likely to be used, as this is damaging to the battery plates.

The handlebar switch positions are slightly different on the battery circuit, the extreme inward, left, position switching on the parking lights. In the non-battery circuits several types of switch are in use but with the same selective positions. The main differences are that the horn is operated either by pressing down the switch lever, or there is a separate horn-button mounted on the switch, Fig. 65. All 150 c.c. models have the switch incorporating a separate horn-button. Individual leads are colour coded for ease of identification.

Where a speedometer bulb is fitted the connexion for it is normally tapped off the terminal plate located in the headlamp and is effectively in parallel with the tail light. In this case the rating of the tail light is reduced from 6 volt 5 watt to 6 volt 3 watt. The speedometer bulb is of the 6 volt 1·5 watt type.

IGNITION AND LIGHTING

A complete specification for the lights is—

125 c.c. STANDARD D OR LD
 Head—6 V 25/25 W (reduce to 15/15 W or 12/12 for better lighting at low speed use)
 Tail—6 V 3 W
  battery—none.

150 c.c. STANDARD D OR LD
 Head—6 V 25/25 W (*see* above)

 Pilot—6 V 5 W
 Tail—6 V 5 W (6 V 3 W with speedo-bulb fitted)
 Speedo-bulb—6 V 1·5 W
  battery—none.

150 c.c. LDB
 Head—6 V 25/25 W
 Pilot—6 V 3 W (or 6 V 1·5 W for increased parking light duration)
 Tail—6 V 3 W (6 V 1·5 W with speedo-bulb fitted)
 Speedo-bulb—6 V 1·5 W
  battery—6 V 4 amp-hr capacity.

SIDECAR MODELS
 use 6 V 3 W tail light and
 6 V 1·5 W tail light on sidecar.

The horn in all cases is operated by A.C. generated by the lighting coil of the magneto, except in the 150 c.c. self-starter models, and is therefore inoperative without the engine running. The engine "stop" or ignition cut-off position is given by extreme movement of the handlebar switch to the right which effectively cuts the high tension output (by earthing the primary circuit) and thus the spark plug receives no current. This position of the switch is spring loaded so that the switch when released will return to the normal "off" position which leaves the ignition circuit connected. Obviously, however, no current can flow through this circuit until the engine is turned over.

Magneto Operation. The principle of magneto operation can be understood by referring to Fig. 66. The two coils are separate and a similar effect is experienced in each. They are attached to a stator or fixed plate and terminate in soft-iron pole-pieces closely matching the shape of the flywheel rim which rotates around them. Inset in the flywheel rim are four bar magnets and as each magnet passes the end of a pole-piece its magnetic field will produce a reaction in the coil, generating in it a surge of electrical current, first in one direction and then in the other. This will occur four times every revolution of the flywheel, thus generating in the lighting coil an alternating current with a frequency four times that of the engine speed.

In the ignition coil, however, only one reversal is used for generation of low-tension current for the ignition circuit since the plug has to spark only once per revolution. To get the necessary high-tension output for the spark to jump the gap between the spark-plug contacts or points, a pair of contacts (points) is inserted in the primary circuit which, when opened, causes a rapid change of current in the primary circuit. This surge is transformed, by mutual induction, into a surge of high voltage in

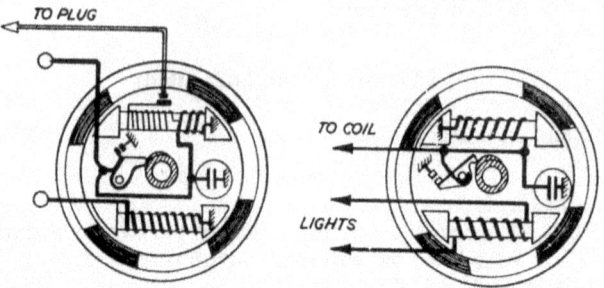

FIG. 66. WIRING CIRCUIT OF THE 125 C.C. FLYWHEEL MAGNETO IS SHOWN ON THE LEFT

The ignition coil incorporates both primary and secondary windings. On the 150 c.c. magneto (Marelli-type, shown on right) the primary of the ignition coil is connected to the primary of an external high-tension coil.

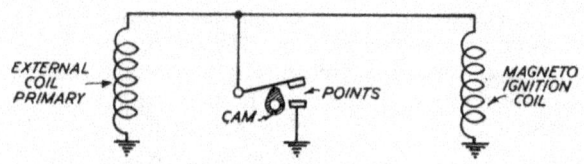

FIG. 67. THE 150 C.C. IGNITION CIRCUIT IS UNIQUE IN THAT THE (IGNITION) GENERATING COIL AND HIGH-TENSION COIL PRIMARY ARE IN SERIES, WITH THE POINTS ACROSS THEM

a secondary coil wound directly on the primary on the 125 c.c. unit. In the 150 c.c. system with separate ignition coil, the system is unique. The magneto ignition coil is connected to the high-tension coil primary and the contact points are across these coils, Fig. 67. In effect, therefore, the high tension primary coil is switched in and out of the primary circuit by means of the contact breaker.

In both cases the surge of high tension in the secondary coil, which is connected direct to the spark plug, is therefore controlled by the opening of the contact points which, in turn, are controlled by a cam on the engine crankshaft. Thus, to "time" the spark correctly for its appearance at the

IGNITION AND LIGHTING 99

plug some 26 degrees before T.D.C., the position of the cam must be correctly arranged with respect to the contact breaker. The cam is effectively fixed in position. The variables are the contact breaker operating arm itself and the position of the flywheel magnets. Thus it is essential that the flywheel rim should be assembled in the correct position. When locked in this position, further small adjustment of the timing is provided for by making it possible to rotate the stator plate of the magneto, carrying the contact breaker assembly, either one way or the other over a small

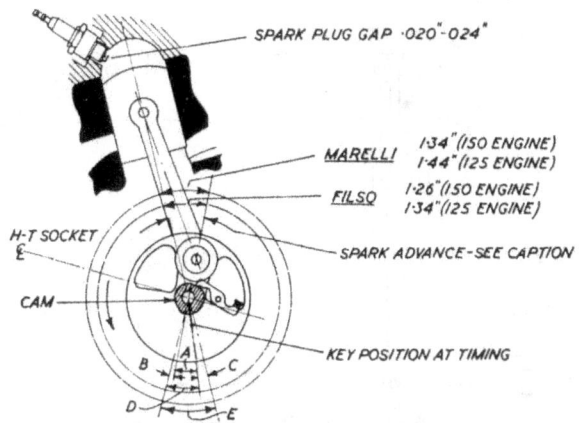

FIG. 68. TIMING DIAGRAM FOR 125 C.C. AND 150 C.C. ENGINES WITH EITHER MARELLI OR FILSO FLYWHEEL MAGNETOS

No figure can be given for points gap since this will vary with adjustment of timing. Spark advance is 26 degrees on 150 c.c. engines and 28 degrees on 125 c.c. engines.

150 c.c. engines	125 c.c. engines
A. 18 degrees.	12 degrees.
B. 4 degrees.	6 degrees.
C. 8 degrees.	22 degrees.
D. 22 degrees.	18 degrees.
E. 30 degrees.	40 degrees.

range. Rotation of the stator clockwise will advance the spark, i.e. cause the plug to fire earlier, and rotation anticlockwise will retard the spark. The possible range of adjustment on the stator plate is a matter of some 20 degrees.

The flywheel is marked with a scribed line on its periphery and, when assembling, this line should correspond with a similar line scribed on the magneto flange with the piston at the T.D.C. position. There is also a further mark on the flywheel rim $1\frac{1}{4}$ in. along in an anticlockwise direction. When this is turned to be opposite the fixed mark on the magneto flange the contact points should be just beginning to open. Actually, the central point of the pull of the magnets on the coil pole pieces occurs at 1¾ in. before T.D.C. (26 degrees) and this can be felt by turning over the flywheel by hand. If necessary, the stator plate can be adjusted to rearrange this setting, then readjusting the contact breaker points to just open at the original setting described (second flywheel mark opposite magneto-flange scribed line). A timing diagram is given in Fig. 68.

On the machine, the coils may readily be identified by their connexions. The function of the condenser is to act as a spark-quench across the contact points and thus prevent undue arcing, as well as contributing to

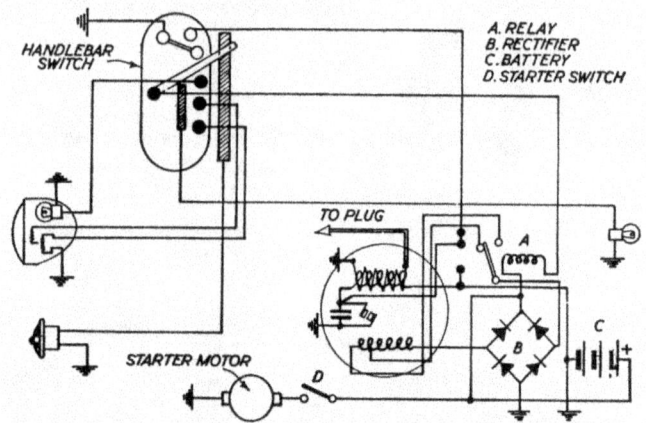

FIG. 69. WIRING DIAGRAM FOR 125 C.C. SELF-STARTER MACHINE (6 VOLTS) WITH RELAY SYSTEM OF CHARGING

the electrical efficiency of the system. The condenser should not be a source of trouble since it is not heavily loaded. The main sources of trouble are badly-adjusted or dirty contact points and broken, bared or partially disconnected leads. Suspected failure of the magneto coils or demagnetization of the magnets are a job for the servicing expert to check or trace. The specific magneto circuits applicable to a particular machine can be traced from Figs. 50–52 and Fig. 66 applied to the appropriate wiring diagram, Figs. 62–4.

Lighting Systems. LDA self-starter models have been produced in a number of variations. The early system applicable to 125 c.c. machines had rectified lighting with charging rate controlled by a moving contact and utilizing a 6-volt battery and 6-volt starter motor. Full-charge rate on this sytem is 3 amps at 30 m.p.h., and 1·5 to 2 amps at "half charge" at this speed. This was later modified by the use of a choke coil as a charge control with the same charge rates as above. A typical system where the charge rate is controlled by a relay is shown in Fig. 69.

IGNITION AND LIGHTING

The 6-volt system was also extended to 150 c.c. machines although only the 12-volt system is likely to be encountered in this country. This employs two 6-volt 13 amp-hr batteries in series and is appreciably different from previous systems in that the entire electrical circuit is fed with direct current instead of alternating current.

The magneto design is modified for increased output in all versions. On the 6-volt circuits the output from the lighting coil is increased from 28 watts to 40 watts. On the 12-volt system a second lighting coil replaces the ignition coil, these two lighting coils being in series, with corresponding

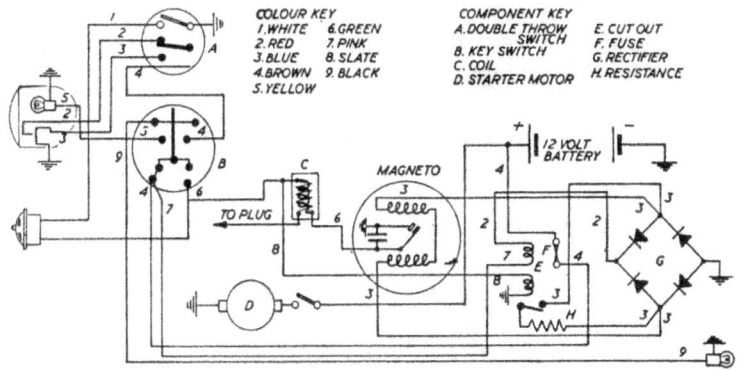

FIG. 70. WIRING DIAGRAM FOR 12-VOLT 150 C.C. LDA SELF-STARTER MODEL

increased output again. The ignition in this case is supplied by battery current and the only function of the lead from the high tension coil to the magneto is to connect to the contact breaker and condenser. A complete wiring diagram is shown in Fig. 70.

In all cases the starter motor is actuated by a lever control on the left-hand handlebar (*see* Figs. 62 and 63). In the 6-volt systems utilizing A.C. for the electrical services the main handlebar switch is of similar form as previously. However, a safety switch is also fitted on the front of the engine compartment, turned by a removable key. This switch disconnects the battery and should always be switched off when the machine is parked. The kick-starter is not fitted to the 125 c.c. self-starter machines, except for later models, but is retained as a standard feature on all 150 c.c. self-starter machines.

On the 12-volt version, the main switch is mounted on the front of the engine compartment and is actuated by a key. The right-hand handlebar switch is then replaced by a smaller double-throw switch which is used only for headlight switching, from main beam to dip, and incorporates the horn-button. The main switch positions are achieved by turning the ignition key in the main switch, Fig. 71. The key can be withdrawn in either the normal "off" or "parking lights" position.

Output from the lighting coils is fed to a plate-type bridge rectifier which supplies D.C. to the battery via a voltage regulator. Maximum output from the rectifier is 4 to 5 amps at 12·5 to 15 volts.

The voltage regulator is a factory set unit and needs no adjustment. It is adjusted to pull in and close its contacts when battery terminal voltage rises to between 14·7 and 15 volts. These contacts then switch in a 3·5 ohm resistance in the generator circuit reducing the current to the battery from 4·5 amps to 1 amp. The cut-out releases, and thus switches out the resistance, when battery terminal voltage falls to between 12·7 and 13 volts.

A fuse is incorporated under the cover of the regulator, or adjacent to it, rated to blow at 8 amps. This will burn out and disconnect the battery

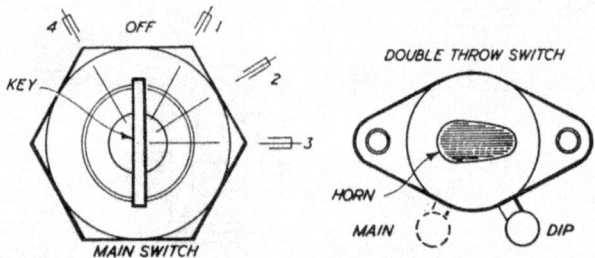

FIG. 71. MAIN (DASHBOARD) AND SECONDARY (HANDLEBAR) SWITCHES ON 12-VOLT LDA MODEL

The main switch is operated by the ignition key.

circuit in the event of a short, or excessive overload, on this circuit, or if the battery is connected the wrong way round, i.e. positive to earth instead of negative to earth. This safeguards the battery. The starter motor lead is independent of this fuse since the current drawn by the electric motor is of the order of 30 amps, but although the starter motor may work the ignition circuit is disconnected until the fault is remedied and the fuse replaced.

Since operation of the starter motor depends on the battery remaining in a good state of charge it is necessary to consider the loading of the electrical supply in winter driving and similar conditions where the lights are used extensively. With specified bulb sizes, output with headlights on is roughly balanced by input at 20 m.p.h. At lower speeds the charge is maintained since the engine speed is necessarily raised by changing down. Current consumption can be worked out by summing the wattage of all the bulbs in use and dividing by the voltage of the battery. Maximum charging rates, achieved at 30 m.p.h. in top gear, can be taken as 4 amps.

If necessary, the machine can be checked in the "static" condition with the engine running and lights switched on. The throttle can be adjusted to give the required speed reading on the speedometer and with an ammeter connected in the brown battery lead, i.e. disconnecting this lead to the battery and reconnecting with the ammeter inserted, the surplus of charge over charge can be measured under different conditions. If a two-way ammeter is used, charge and discharge characteristics can be observed.

To reduce the demand on the system, should this be necessary, the wattage rating of the headlight bulb can be reduced. Recommended values for all the bulbs on self-starter machines are—

150 c.c. LDA—12-VOLT SYSTEM

Head—12 V 25/25 W
Pilot—12 V 3 W
Tail—12 V 3 W (reduce to 1·5 W with speedo-bulb)
Speedo—12 V 1·5 W
    battery—12 V 13 amp-hr capacity.

THE SPARKING PLUG

The sparking plug is described separately since, although this is a standard commercial component, the performance of a two-stroke engine operating on petroil mixture is largely dependent on the characteristics of the plug. Most starting and running troubles are traceable either to a faulty plug or a plug of incorrect type.

The quality of the spark itself is readily checked by turning the engine over with the high-tension lead disconnected and held $\frac{3}{16}$ to $\frac{1}{4}$ in. away from the engine casing. A good spark here, however, is no automatic guarantee of a good spark across the plug points under compression in the engine.

The greater the gap between the spark plug points the greater the high-tension voltage required to bridge this gap. Under compression, the gap is effectively ten times as large as in air; thus, a $\frac{1}{4}$ in. spark in air would bridge only a $0.25 \div 10$ or 0.025 in. gap in the engine under working conditions. A maximum setting of 0.020 in. is recommended, but this will have a tendency to grow. Hence the need to remove the plug and check the spark gap at regular intervals, and to reset when necessary.

For proper operation, too, the spark for igniting the fuel mixture must maintain or reach the proper temperature. The temperature at which the mixture ignites depends largely on the compression ratio. In the Lambretta engine a minimum point temperature of about 500 degrees centigrade is required to ensure that the points are hot enough to volatilize the oil in the mixture and not allow it to collect on the points and so foul them. Solid fuel of this nature tends to act as an insulator, which is the primary reason why a cold, flooded engine will not start. The plug points are saturated with fuel. The upper limit of point temperature is about 850 degrees centigrade. If this temperature is reached the fuel mixture will self-ignite independently of the spark. Thus, apart from the actual *spark* temperature it will be appreciated that the temperature which the spark plug itself maintains is of equal significance. Once this is understood it will readily be appreciated that a plug can be too "hot" or too "cold," although these characteristics are correctly referred to as "soft" or "hard," respectively (*see* Chapters IV and V).

APPENDIX

SPECIFICATION
(Models D, LD and LDA)

Overall length. 70 in.
Overall height (no windscreen). 38 in.
Ground clearance. 4⅜ in.
Handlebar width. 29 in.
Wheelbase. 50½ in.
Unloaded weight. Model D 165 lb; model LD 194 lb; model LDA 210 lb.
Tyres. 4·00 × 8 (on interchangeable split rims).
Engine. 125 c.c., bore 52 mm (2·047 in.); stroke 58 mm (2·283 in.); displacement 123 c.c.; B.H.P., 5 B.H.P. at 5,000 r.p.m.; compression ratio 6·5:1.
150 c.c., bore 57 mm (2·244 in.); stroke 58 mm (2·283 in.); displacement 148 c.c.; B.H.P., 6 B.H.P. at 4,800 r.p.m.; compression ratio 6·5:1.
Single cylinder two-stroke engines air-cooled by magneto-fan draught.
Magneto ignition. Setting before T.D.C. 26 degrees (150 c.c.); 28 degrees (125 c.c.); contact breaker gap variable according to timing setting.
Gearbox ratios. First, 12·9:1; second 7·5:1; third (top) 4·75:1. Constant mesh gearbox with hand control combined with clutch control.
Clutch. Multiplate in oil bath (3 driven plates); release stroke, 5 mm; free length 22 mm length under 6 kg (13¼ lb) 10 mm.
Transmission. Shaft.
Carburettor. Dell'Orto; choke 19 mm; main jet 72 (maximum 100); needle jet 255B; pilot jet 40 (*see also* Chapter VI, Section 12).
Magneto-generator. Marelli or Filso (four-pole); standard output 28 watt (C, D, and LD models), 40 watt (LDA model).
Spark plug. Champion L11S, K.L.G. F80, Lodge HH14; spark plug gap 0·015 to 0·020 in.
Brakes. Front, cable operated 125 mm dia. × 15 mm width; rear, cable operated 140 mm dia. × 20 mm width (except C, LC, and early 125 c.c. D and LD models).
Frame. Single beam type, steel tube section; rake angle, 23 degrees.
Forks. Front suspension by two rocker and two coil springs in grease-tight units (D, LD and LDA models); rear, suspension by torsion bar and hydraulic damper (D, LD and LDA models).

Tyre pressures. Front, 15–16 lb sq in.; rear, 22–24 lb sq in.; sidecar version, 25 lb sq in. all wheels.

Fuel. Petrol-oil mixture ($\frac{1}{2}$ pt SAE 30 oil per gal of standard petrol).

Tank capacity. Model D, 1·4 gal plus 1·25 pt reserve; models LD and LDA 1·55 gal plus 1·25 pt reserve.

Oil. Gearbox: winter, $\frac{3}{4}$ pt SAE 20; summer, $\frac{3}{4}$ pt SAE 30; rear axle, $\frac{1}{4}$ pt SAE 140.

Kick-starter ratio (pedal to crankshaft). 13·3:1.

Lights. Models D and LD, 6 volt 25/25 watt, 6 volt 5 watt; model LDA, headlamp 12 volt 25/25 watt bifilament, 12 volt 3 watt pilot, tail 12 volt 3 watt, speedometer 12 volt 1·5 watt. (*See also* Chapter VII.)

INDEX

Air—
  filter, 88
  leaks, 88
Automatic—
  advance/retard, 84

BATTERY, 48
Brake—
  adjustment, 47, 60–2
  removal, 66, 67
Brakes, 24, 37, 60, 66,

Bulb sizes, 96, 97, 103

CABLES, 46, 59–66
Carburettor, 14, 18, 19, 86–9
Charging, 95

Clutch, 20, 21, 22, 73–5
  adjustment, 47, 73–5
Colour schemes, 10
Compression ratio, 15
Connecting rod, 11, 12, 85
Controls, 27–30
Cornering, 34–6
Crankpin, 11, 12, 85
Crankshaft, 11, 12, 84–6
Crown wheel, 79, 80
Cruising speeds, 7
Cylinder, 11, 12, 84–6

DASHBOARD switch, 102
Decarbonizing, 50, 67–8
Dell'Orto carburettor, 86, 87, 89

ELECTRICAL circuits—
  125 c.c. D and LD, 93
  125 c.c. self-starter, 100
  150 c.c., 94
  LDA, 101
  LDB, 95
  magneto, 98
Engine, principles, 11

Equipment, 9, 10

FAULTS, 55–8
Filso magneto, 82, 83, 84
Final drive, 79–82
Flywheel, 99. *See also* Magneto
Frame specification, 105
Front forks, 89, 90
Fuel—
  capacity, 8
  consumption, 8
  mixture, 39

GEAR changing, 32, 33
Gearbox, 22, 23, 24, 77–9
  ratios, 105
Gudgeon pin, 11, 12, 85

HANDLEBARS, 89
  switches, 96, 101, 102

IGNITION—
  circuits—*see* Electrical circuits
  coil, 82, 83, 93, 98, 101
  timing, 15, 99

JETS, 88. *See also* Carburettors

KICKSTARTER, 24, 70–72

LAMBRETTA model—
  A, 3
  B, 3
  C, 2, 3, 5
  D, 4, 5, 8, 9
  LC, 3, 5
  LD, 4, 5, 6, 8, 9
  LDA, 9
  LDB, 7, 9

Lighting coil, 82–3, 93, 94, 98, 101
Lights, 97, 100–3. *See also* Electrical circuits

Lubrication, 40, 42
  table 41

MAGNETO, 16, 17, 82–4, 97–100
  Marelli, 82–4

Monthly maintenance, 46

PARKING lights, 94, 95
Pilot light, 93
Piston, 11, 12, 85
  rings, 15, 16, 85

RECTIFIER, 96
Relay, 100
Removing wheel—
  front, 51–4
  rear, 66, 67

Running-in, 33, 34

SELF-STARTER, 90–2
Sidecar, 7
Silencer, 68–70
Six-monthly maintenance, 49
Spark timing, 15, 99
Sparking plug, 13, 45, 103–4
Specification, 105-6
Speedometer, 81
  bulb, 95, 96
Starting, 30, 31, 32

Suspension—
  front, 26, 90
  rear, 25

TAXATION, 8, 9
Three-monthly maintenance, 49
Throttle needle, 88
Timing diagram, 99
Tools, 59, 60, 61
Torsion bar, 25, 75–7
Transmission—
  B, C, and LC, 78
  D, LD, 77
Twist grip, 62–5
Tyre—
  pressures, 44
  removing, 52

VOLTAGE regulator, 102

WEEKLY maintenance, 44
Wheel nuts, 48
Wheels, removing, 51–4, 66–7
Wiring diagrams—
  125 D and LD, 93
  125 LDA, 101
  125 c.c. self-starter, 100
  150 c.c. D, 94
  LDB, 95
  magneto, 98

ZENITH carburettor, 86, 89

The noted folk singer BURL IVES on his LAMBRETTA

OTHER CLASSIC MOTORCYCLE MANUALS CURRENTLY AVAILABLE

ARIEL WORKSHOP MANUAL 1933-1951:
All single, twin & 4 cylinder models

ARIEL (BOOK OF) MAINTENANCE & REPAIR MANUAL 1932-1939:
LF3, LF4, LG, NF3, NF4, NG, OG, VA, VA3, VA4, VB, VF3, VF4, VG, Red Hunter LH, NH, OH, VH & Square Four 4F, 4G, 4H

BMW FACTORY WORKSHOP MANUAL R27, R28:
English, German, French and Spanish text

BMW FACTORY WORKSHOP MANUAL R50, R50S, R60, R69S:
Also includes a supplement for the USA models: R50US, R60US, R69US. English, German, French and Spanish text

BSA (BOOK OF) MAINTENANCE & REPAIR 1936-1939:
All Pre-War single & twin cylinder SV & OHV models through 1939
150cc, 250cc, 350cc, 500cc, 600cc, 750cc & 1,000cc

DUCATI OHC FACTORY WORKSHOP MANUAL:
160 Junior Monza, 250 Monza, 250 GT, 250 Mark 3, 250 Mach 1, 250 SCR & 350 Sebring

HONDA 250 & 305cc FACTORY WORKSHOP MANUAL:
C.72 C.77 CS.72, CS.77, CB.72, CB.77 [HAWK]

HONDA 125 & 150cc FACTORY WORKSHOP MANUAL:
C.92, CS.92, CB.92, C.95 & CA.95

HONDA 50cc FACTORY WORKSHOP MANUAL: C.100

HONDA 50cc FACTORY WORKSHOP MANUAL: C.110

HONDA (BOOK OF) MAINTENANCE & REPAIR 1960-1966:
50cc C.100, C.102, C.110 & C.114 ~ 125cc C.92 & CB.92
250cc C.72 & CB.72 ~ 305cc CB.77

LAMBRETTA (BOOK OF) MAINTENANCE & REPAIR:
125 & 150cc, all models up to 1958, except model "48".

NORTON FACTORY TWIN CYLINDER WORKSHOP MANUAL
1957-1970: *Lightweight Twins:* 250cc Jubilee, 350cc Navigator and 400cc Electra and the *Heavyweight Twins:* Model 77, 88, 88SS, 99, 99SS, Sports Special, Manxman, Mercury, Atlas, G15, P11, N15, Ranger (P11A).

NORTON (BOOK OF) MAINTENANCE & REPAIR 1932-1939:
All Pre-War SV, OHV and OHC models: 16H, 16I, 18, 19, 20, 50, 55, ES2, CJ, CSI, International 30 & 40

SUZUKI 200 & 250cc FACTORY WORKSHOP MANUAL:
250cc T20 [X-6 Hustler] ~ 200cc T200 [X-5 Invader & Sting Ray Scrambler]

SUZUKI 250cc FACTORY WORKSHOP MANUAL: 250cc ~ T10

TRIUMPH (BOOK OF) MAINTENANCE & REPAIR 1935-1939:
All Pre-War single & twin cylinder models: L2/1, 2/1, 2/5, 3/1, 3/2, 3/5, 5/1, 5/2, 5/3, 5/4, 5/5, 5/10, 6/1, Tiger 70, 80, 90 & 2H. Tiger 70C, 3S & 3H, Tiger 80C & 5H, Tiger 90C, 6S, 2HC & 3SC, 5T Speed Twin & 5S and T100 Tiger 100

TRIUMPH 1937-1951 WORKSHOP MANUAL (A. St. J. Masters):
Covers rigid frame and sprung hub single cylinder SV & OHV and twin cylinder OHV pre-war, military, and post-war models

TRIUMPH 1945-1955 FACTORY WORKSHOP MANUAL NO.11:
Covers pre-unit, twin-cylinder rigid frame, sprung hub, swing-arm and 350cc, 500cc & 650cc.

VESPA (BOOK OF) MAINTENANCE & REPAIR 1946-1959:
All 125cc & 150cc models including 42/L2 & Gran Sport

VINCENT WORKSHOP MANUAL 1935-1955:
All Series A, B & C Models

COMING SOON IN THIS SAME SERIES:

BRIDGESTONE FACTORY WORKSHOP MANUAL: 50 Sport, 60 Sport, 90 De Luxe, 90 Trail, 90 Mountain, 90 Sport, 175 Dual Twin & Hurricane

BRITISH MILITARY MAINTENANCE & REPAIR MANUAL:
Service & Repair data for all British WD motorcycles

BRITISH MOTORCYCLE ENGINES: AJS, Ariel, BSA, Excelsior, JAP, Norton, Royal Enfield, Rudge, Scott, Sunbeam, Triumph, Velocette, Villiers & Vincent ~ a compilation of 1950's articles from *The Motor Cycle* dealing with engine design.

CEZETTA 175cc MODEL 501 MANUAL & PARTS BOOK

VILLIERS ENGINE WORKSHOP MANUAL:
All Villiers engines and ancillaries through 1947

PLEASE CHECK OUR WEBSITE FOR AVAILABILITY
~ WWW.VELOCEPRESS.COM ~

www.ingramcontent.com/pod-product-compliance
Lightning Source LLC
Chambersburg PA
CBHW070559170426
43201CB00012B/1878